The Exit Plan

The Exit Plan

How Smart Founders Build With Selling in Mind

Jonathan Mercer

Mindful Pages

Published in 2025

ISBN: 9789374122235 (PB)
ISBN: 9789374121702 (eBook)

Published by

Mindful Pages
Imprint of Alpha Editions LLC
312 W. 2nd St #1834
Casper, WY 82601, USA

This book was developed using advanced writing tools to support the drafting and ideation process. All content has been thoughtfully curated, refined, and reviewed to ensure quality and relevance.

Content

Introduction viii

Chapter 1 The Myth of Forever Ownership 1

Chapter 2 Defining Value Beyond Profit 22

Chapter 3 Systems as the Silent Valuator 42

Chapter 4 Building Investor Readiness.............................. 63

Chapter 5 Designing Leadership That Lasts 86

Chapter 6 Timing the Market and Yourself..................... 104

Chapter 7 Negotiating the Legacy 121

Chapter 8 Designing Backwards From Day One............ 140

Chapter 9 Freedom, Not Finish Line 161

About the Author 178

Introduction

The story is told of a nineteenth-century industrialist who, at the height of his power, summoned his children and declared: *"This factory is not my life's work—it is your inheritance, and one day, it must belong to strangers."* The remark puzzled his heirs. How could the very creation that defined his identity be destined, almost deliberately, for relinquishment? Yet the industrialist was right. Within a generation, the business had passed into the hands of outsiders, surviving and growing precisely because he had designed it to outlast him. His foresight was not romantic resignation but strategy. He understood what many entrepreneurs—then and now—struggle to accept: a business becomes enduring when it is prepared to be let go.

Every founder dreams of freedom, but most end up bound more tightly than any employee. What begins as a vision of autonomy—a refusal to answer to a boss, a longing to create something on one's own terms—too often calcifies into captivity. The emails multiply, the payroll expands, the product demands evolve. The founder who once imagined liberation through enterprise wakes each day to find the business now dictates their time, their identity, their very sense of worth. This is the paradox at the heart of entrepreneurship: the pursuit of freedom gives birth to a new form of servitude.

And yet, there is another paradox, more hidden, more decisive. The companies that outlive their founders, that generate wealth across decades, are rarely those clung to with possessive zeal. They are the ones conceived with detachment in mind, designed from the outset to be sold, transferred, or passed on. This book insists that exit planning is not a disloyal afterthought but the architecture of strategy itself. To build with selling in mind is not to diminish passion; it is to protect it from turning toxic.

The reluctance to plan for departure is not a quirk of poor management. It is a cultural blind spot. Across entrepreneurial communities, to sell one's business is often whispered about as "selling out," a betrayal of staff, customers, or one's own vision. Stories of heroic founders immortalised in control—think of Jobs, Bezos, or Branson—dominate our imagination, obscuring the fact that the majority of enduring enterprises were shaped by a disciplined readiness to hand over the reins. The Roman merchants of antiquity, who treated succession as part of their accounting; the Renaissance trading families, who embedded continuity into their charters; the twentieth-century dynasties who professionalised management structures—all recognised that departure was not the end of ownership but the condition of legacy.

The result of ignoring this truth is plain. Every year, thousands of businesses collapse not because their product failed or their market disappeared, but because their founder refused to envision the end. The wreckage is more than financial. Families are destabilised, employees scattered, and communities deprived of services once integral to their identity. To neglect the exit is to court ruin, however brilliant the beginnings.

This book was written to confront that blind spot head-on. It unites the insights of investors, who understand what makes a business transferable; psychologists, who study why identity becomes entangled with ownership; and historians, who reveal how the most durable institutions were constructed with foresight. It offers both a corrective and a promise: founders who design for exit from the start can enjoy enterprises that are more profitable in the present and more resilient in the future.

At stake here is not only the personal wealth of entrepreneurs but the very texture of economic life. Small and mid-sized businesses account for the majority of employment in most nations. When they crumble with their founders, communities bear the loss. When they thrive beyond a single individual, society gains stability, innovation, and generational prosperity. The matter of exit is thus not merely private but public. It concerns how wealth circulates, how knowledge persists, how communities sustain themselves when charismatic figures inevitably step aside.

The motif that will recur throughout this book is that of architecture. A building is not designed to be occupied by its architect forever; it is made to house lives unknown, to accommodate futures unseen. So too with businesses. To build without planning for exit is like constructing a house without doors. The structure may rise, impressive at first glance, but it traps its inhabitants until they either break free or suffocate within. To design with departure in mind, by contrast, is to ensure permeability, adaptability, and endurance.

What does this architecture of exit look like in practice? It begins with confronting myths. The first chapters address the deep psychological resistance to imagining the end, the stigma attached to selling, and the historical precedents that expose this resistance as both modern and misguided. From there, the focus shifts to value—what it truly means, beyond mere profit, and how buyers perceive it differently than founders. Systems, documentation, leadership succession, market timing: each theme is a pillar in the structure of a business capable of surviving transition.

The urgency of this subject cannot be overstated. We live in an age where markets pivot with alarming speed, where technological disruption shortens product cycles, and where investor appetites fluctuate with global shocks. The founder who waits for the "perfect" moment to sell is like a sailor waiting for the sea to still: paralysis ensures shipwreck. At the same time, the private strain on entrepreneurs has never been more visible. Burnout, disillusionment, even despair often follow when passion alone is asked to bear the burden of a business that has no clear future beyond its founder.

Against this backdrop, *The Exit Plan* proposes a different vision of entrepreneurial freedom. Freedom not as perpetual control, but as deliberate release. Freedom not as ownership chained indefinitely, but as the ability to step away knowing the creation will live on. This freedom requires courage, for it forces founders to separate their worth from their enterprise, their identity from their product. But it also offers relief: the possibility of enjoying the fruits of labour without being consumed by them.

This book asks uncomfortable questions. Why do so many of us equate selling with betrayal? What happens to our sense of self when the company no longer requires us? Can one preserve culture, brand, and mission after handing over the keys? And perhaps most challenging: might our truest legacy as founders be measured not by how long we hold on, but by how gracefully we let go?

The chapters that follow will not offer formulaic checklists or empty reassurances. They will demand reflection as much as action, challenging cherished assumptions while equipping you with pragmatic tools. The reward is not only financial preparedness but a transformation in perspective: to see yourself not merely as an operator trapped within the machine, but as an architect of something greater, something built to endure.

The exit is not a finish line. It is a passage. Those who approach it with foresight and humility find not an ending but a beginning—the rediscovery of freedom, the possibility of reinvention, the knowledge that their creation stands strong without them. This book is your guide to designing that passage from day one.

Chapter 1
The Myth of Forever Ownership

On a winter's morning in 2016, the founder of a celebrated London fashion label arrived at her studio to discover the locks had been changed. Investors had seized control overnight. For two decades she had poured herself into the company—her aesthetic, her values, her very identity stitched into every seam. Yet when the financial scaffolding collapsed, so did her sense of self. "It was as though they had taken my name from me," she later reflected. The company survived in some form, but for her it was as if she had been erased. The episode is more than a cautionary tale of corporate politics; it illuminates a deeper truth. Many entrepreneurs do not merely run their businesses—they become their businesses. And when that conflation of self and enterprise is threatened, it destabilises everything: strategy, judgement, and eventually survival.

This belief—that a business is something to be held forever—is rarely articulated outright, yet it hums beneath the surface of countless decisions. Founders who might be ruthlessly pragmatic in negotiations suddenly turn sentimental when faced with the idea of relinquishing control. The numbers may point one way; the heart insists another. Behind this tension lies a profound psychological attachment. To build is to create; to create is to invest identity. And so, when asked to imagine an exit, many recoil as though asked to amputate a limb.

The paradox is striking. The very act of ownership, which promises agency and autonomy, can cloud the clarity needed to protect the creation itself. Psychologists call it the "endowment effect": once something is ours, we value it disproportionately, even irrationally. For founders, the effect is magnified a hundredfold. A business is not a painting purchased at auction; it is the canvas, the paint, and the hand that wielded the brush. How could such a thing ever be priced, let alone sold? Yet it must be, if it is to outlive its maker.

There is, of course, a harsher cultural script at play. In many entrepreneurial circles, selling is branded as betrayal. To let go is to abandon ship, to cash out at the expense of loyal staff and devoted customers. The phrase "selling out" carries venom; it implies greed, cowardice, disloyalty. Founders internalise this stigma, often subconsciously, and it distorts their choices. Deals that could secure the future of the business are declined out of fear of judgement. Leaders postpone succession planning lest they be accused of losing faith. Ironically, what is framed as loyalty to the business can become the very act that imperils it.

This stigma is not new. History is filled with figures celebrated for their unwavering grip—titans who appeared inseparable from their empires. Yet for every Steve Jobs or Henry Ford, there are hundreds of quieter, less mythologised founders who safeguarded their legacies precisely by preparing to let go. The cultural narratives we elevate—of heroic founders who never release control—are selective retellings. They glorify the exception, not the rule. And they obscure the pragmatic truth: most businesses that endure across generations do so because exit, succession, or sale was baked into their DNA.

Consider the merchant families of Renaissance Florence. To them, succession was not an afterthought but a cornerstone of commerce. Charters detailed how authority would transfer, how apprentices would inherit responsibilities, how partnerships could be dissolved and reformed. These merchants understood that wealth was fragile unless it was structured to outlast the founder's mortality. Centuries later, conglomerates like Mitsubishi and Tata institutionalised the same foresight, embedding systems of governance that allowed leadership to rotate while preserving the enterprise. Their lesson is simple yet profound: businesses designed for succession endure; those built only for possession wither.

Contrast this with modern cautionary tales. Family-owned restaurants that collapse when the patriarch refuses to cede the kitchen. Start-ups that crumble when their visionary founder insists on micromanagement until burnout erodes the company's foundations. Global firms that unravel because succession was delayed until crisis forced hasty, ill-prepared handovers. The cost of ignoring the end is rarely just financial. It is emotional exhaustion, fractured relationships, wasted potential. The founder's refusal to imagine departure becomes the business's downfall.

This chapter begins by probing the psychological roots of ownership attachment—why founders struggle so intensely to imagine the end. It then turns to the stigma of selling out, exploring how cultural narratives distort our perception of success and why reframing sale as achievement is not merely semantic but existential. We will then step back into history, tracing how some of the world's most enduring enterprises were intentionally structured to pass beyond their originators. Finally, we will confront the cost of denial, examining businesses that ignored succession until it was too late.

To read these sections is not to encounter abstract theory. It is to confront the living dynamics that shape whether a business thrives or perishes. The founder who sees their company as an extension of their soul must reckon with the fact that soul and structure are not the same. The leader who equates selling with betrayal must ask: is refusing to prepare not the greater betrayal? The student of history must decide whether to emulate myths of eternal ownership or the quieter wisdom of foresight.

The myth of forever ownership is seductive, flattering even. It tells the founder they are indispensable, that their identity and enterprise are one. But myths can suffocate as easily as they inspire. To dismantle this illusion is not to diminish the romance of entrepreneurship; it is to preserve it. What follows is an invitation to look unflinchingly at the end—not as defeat, but as design. Turn the page, and the first illusions will begin to crack.

Why We Struggle to Imagine the End

On a summer afternoon in Silicon Valley, a venture capitalist once asked a young founder what his ultimate ambition for the company was. The investor expected to hear about IPOs, mergers, or strategic acquisitions. Instead, the founder smiled and said, "I'll be running this company until I die." He meant it as a declaration of commitment, but the room fell silent. For the investor, it was not devotion but a warning sign: a leader unable—or unwilling—to imagine an end was also a leader unlikely to make rational decisions when opportunity or necessity demanded them.

This refusal to picture the end is not confined to starry-eyed entrepreneurs. It is one of the deepest instincts of ownership. We struggle to imagine parting with what we have built, not because it is financially unsound but because it feels existentially unthinkable. To the founder, the business is not just a commercial entity. It is an identity, a legacy, a biography written in balance sheets and customer testimonials. Handing it over can feel akin to erasing the self.

Psychologists have long recognised this pattern. The *endowment effect*—the tendency to assign higher value to what we already possess—shows up in experiments where people refuse to sell an ordinary mug for twice what they would have paid to buy it. In entrepreneurship, this bias magnifies beyond recognition. A business represents not a trivial object but years of sacrifice, sleepless nights, and emotional investment. To ask a founder to assign a market price to that is to ask them to quantify their very sense of worth. Unsurprisingly, many overestimate value, reject reasonable offers, and cling to ownership until circumstances make the decision for them.

There is also the phenomenon of *identity fusion*, a term used by social psychologists to describe how individuals merge their personal identity with a group or institution. Soldiers often experience it with their regiments; religious leaders with their faith communities. Founders fuse with their companies. The brand becomes a mirror of the self, the employees an extension of the family, the headquarters a physical manifestation of their will. To let go of the company is to fracture the self-image. Small wonder the mind resists the very thought.

Yet this attachment, however understandable, clouds judgement. Rational strategy requires perspective: the ability to weigh risks, opportunities, and timing with some detachment. But detachment is precisely what many founders lack. They mistake loyalty for vision. They tell themselves they are safeguarding the company's future when, in fact, they are safeguarding their own sense of indispensability. The two are not the same. A company can thrive without its founder; a founder can thrive without perpetual ownership. But as long as the myth of forever ownership persists, both risk collapse.

The emotional undercurrents are reinforced by cultural ones. Society loves the story of the founder who never lets go, who dies at the helm, who remains forever intertwined with the brand. Think of the mythology surrounding Walt Disney, Steve Jobs, or Coco Chanel—figures who loom so large that it is difficult to imagine their companies without them. These stories, endlessly repeated, distort our sense of normalcy. For every Jobs, there are thousands of founders who wisely sold, stepped aside, or transitioned gracefully. Their stories receive less fanfare precisely because they lack the drama of eternal possession. Quiet foresight does not make for mythic legend, yet it is the bedrock of resilience.

In many cultures, especially those with strong familial or artisanal traditions, letting go is framed as betrayal. The business is the family's honour, the manifestation of loyalty to staff and community. To sell it is seen as desertion, to delegate control as weakness. This stigma compels founders to cling longer than is prudent, even when opportunities beckon. The irony is painful: in refusing to "betray" the company by imagining its end, they may condemn it to death by neglect.

Consider the restaurant that closes its doors when its ageing owner insists no one else can replicate the recipes. Or the craftsman who never trains apprentices, leaving customers adrift when illness strikes. These are not failures of product or market; they are failures of imagination. The inability to envisage an end blinds leaders to continuity. And continuity, not eternal ownership, is the true marker of legacy.

Philosophers have wrestled with this impulse for centuries. The Stoics warned against attachment, urging recognition that all possessions are temporary, all roles transient. To cling is to suffer. Yet modern entrepreneurship often glorifies the opposite: the founder as eternal monarch, inseparable from the creation. The contradiction is stark. We revere innovation yet cling to permanence; we praise disruption yet resist disruption of the self. The founder who cannot imagine an ending is like an author who refuses to write the final chapter, leaving the story unfinished until others discard it.

And yet there is a subtler dimension: mortality. To plan for the end of one's business is to confront the end of oneself. Many founders prefer the illusion of continuity—the belief that as long as the business endures under their control, they too remain vital. Succession planning becomes an unwelcome reminder of finitude. Better, the mind insists, not to look too far ahead. But denial is a fragile defence. Time, markets, and biology eventually enforce their own deadlines.

The challenge, then, is to separate identity from ownership. A founder is not reducible to their business, however intertwined. Their creativity, their courage, their capacity to build—these are not extinguished by selling or stepping aside. On the contrary, they can be liberated. But such liberation requires a mental shift, a willingness to imagine an end without equating it with erasure.

The paradox remains unresolved. On the one hand, attachment provides the passion and resilience necessary to endure the arduous years of building. On the other, unchecked attachment clouds the vision needed to protect the company's future. To disentangle the two is no small feat. It demands discipline, foresight, and sometimes the humility to admit that others may steer better in seasons ahead.

The question lingers, deliberately unresolved: what is the true legacy of a founder—the length of time they cling to their creation, or the strength with which that creation endures without them? Until one confronts this tension, the myth of forever ownership will continue to seduce, and destroy, in equal measure.

The Stigma of Selling Out

When Ben & Jerry's was acquired by Unilever in 2000, headlines accused the ice cream pioneers of betraying their hippie ideals. For decades, the Vermont-based company had cultivated an image of countercultural authenticity: fair trade ingredients, environmental activism, and a community-first ethos. The sale to a multinational conglomerate, critics said, was proof that even the most principled brands would eventually bow to corporate greed. But inside the deal, the story was more complicated. Ben Cohen and Jerry Greenfield secured legal provisions to protect the company's social mission, creating one of the first models for "double bottom line" acquisitions. They had not sold out; they had negotiated continuity. Yet the narrative of betrayal stuck, a reminder of how deeply culture resists the idea that founders might leave on their own terms.

This reflex to treat selling as a form of desertion has roots in a broader cultural mythology. Across much of the entrepreneurial world, founders are revered as visionaries, stewards, and even guardians of their creations. To walk away, it is assumed, is to abandon not only a business but also a community of employees, customers, and ideals. The language itself reveals the bias. We call it "selling out" rather than "cashing in," "handing over," or even "graduating." The connotation is moral rather than financial: the founder has sinned against some unwritten code of loyalty.

Yet the paradox is glaring. If a founder secures the future of the business by finding it a stable new owner, have they betrayed it—or honoured it? When a parent entrusts a child to a capable school or guardian, we do not call it abandonment. We call it care. Why then do we vilify entrepreneurs for recognising their own limits and seeking continuity beyond themselves? The answer lies not in the logic of commerce but in the narratives we tell about leadership, sacrifice, and permanence.

Part of the stigma comes from the archetype of the heroic founder. Our collective imagination favours stories of singular individuals who defy the odds, cling to their vision, and remain at the helm until death or disaster. Henry Ford is remembered as the stubborn industrialist who refused to relinquish control; Steve Jobs as the obsessive perfectionist inseparable from Apple's DNA. These figures are mythologised precisely because of their intransigence.

Their identities fused so completely with their companies that we celebrate them as inseparable. Against this backdrop, selling appears cowardly, as though the founder lacked the fortitude to endure.

But such myths are selective and misleading. They obscure the quieter stories of founders who exited wisely and preserved their legacies. Consider Ingvar Kamprad, who built IKEA into a global phenomenon by deliberately separating his personal control from the company's governance. Through a complex foundation structure, he ensured continuity beyond himself, long before his retirement. Or James Dyson, who has openly acknowledged that succession and future ownership must be planned, even if such planning eventually requires relinquishment. These stories rarely make headlines because foresight lacks the drama of downfall. But they are, in fact, the norm among enterprises that endure.

The stigma is also intensified by cultural context. In founder-driven societies—family businesses in Italy, community enterprises in Japan, or start-ups in America's tech hubs—identity and loyalty are intertwined. Selling is often framed not as a financial strategy but as treason against kinship or community. In Japan, where concepts of stewardship and continuity dominate, founders often prefer to adopt heirs rather than sell, even if external acquisition would better secure the company's future. In the United States, where entrepreneurial grit is idolised, the notion of "cashing out" carries undertones of greed, especially if employees or customers fear being abandoned. The stigma may take different shapes, but it carries the same moral charge: selling equals disloyalty.

At its core, this perception conflates *control* with *commitment*. We assume that only by retaining ownership can a founder remain true to the mission. But this is a fallacy. Commitment can take other forms: designing contracts that protect values, establishing leadership pipelines, or ensuring cultural continuity through governance structures. Ben & Jerry's insistence on a mission-driven board is one example. Another is Patagonia, which recently transferred ownership into a trust designed to preserve its environmental mission indefinitely. Both cases illustrate that relinquishing equity does not mean abandoning ideals. It can, paradoxically, be the most effective way to protect them.

The stigma also persists because selling exposes an uncomfortable truth about ambition. We prefer to imagine that businesses are eternal, that visions can be preserved intact, that founders will remain forever at the helm. Exit disrupts this fantasy. It forces recognition of limits—of time, mortality, and the inevitability of change. For employees, it can trigger anxieties about job security; for customers, fears of declining quality; for communities, doubts about continuity. These anxieties often coalesce into moral judgement: the founder has "sold out," and the future is uncertain. Yet the real betrayal is not the sale itself but the failure to prepare stakeholders for it. When exit is abrupt, opaque, or profit-driven alone, the stigma becomes self-fulfilling.

Reframing selling as success requires a shift in narrative. Instead of treating exit as abandonment, we might view it as graduation: the point at which a founder has built something robust enough to survive without them. In this sense, the sale is proof of achievement, not betrayal. Investors recognise this logic instinctively: a company that attracts buyers is, by definition, a company with transferable value. Customers may even benefit if new ownership brings stability, resources, or innovation. Employees may gain security if succession prevents collapse. The founder, too, gains freedom—freedom to reinvest, to create anew, or simply to rest.

Still, the stigma lingers. It is sustained not only by cultural mythologies but also by the founder's own psychology. To admit that selling is acceptable requires disentangling self-worth from ownership, pride from possession. It is no small task. Many resist until forced by crisis, at which point the sale becomes reactive rather than strategic. By then, the stigma attaches more easily, because the sale looks like desperation rather than foresight.

The challenge, then, is to reclaim the narrative. To speak of selling not as surrender but as stewardship. To highlight stories where exit preserved rather than destroyed value. To remind founders that permanence of ownership is not the ultimate measure of success; continuity of impact is.

And here lies the lingering question, deliberately unresolved: what if the true betrayal is not in selling, but in clinging too long? What if the act of honouring one's creation means preparing to step away, even at the cost of judgement? Until we confront this inversion, the stigma of selling out will persist, and with it, countless founders will mistake loyalty for longevity—at the expense of both.

What History's Founders Knew

In the guildhalls of Renaissance Florence, merchants drafted contracts that extended beyond their own lifetimes. They arranged for apprentices to inherit partnerships, codified family rights in business charters, and created financial instruments to safeguard enterprises against the chaos of succession. These men, who dealt daily in wool, banking, and shipping, lived in a world where plague and war could end a life abruptly. Yet they understood a truth often forgotten by modern entrepreneurs: if an enterprise was to endure, it had to be designed to survive its founder. The paradox is striking. We think of pre-modern commerce as fragile and personality-driven, yet many of these merchants displayed a structural foresight that makes some of today's start-ups look amateur by comparison.

Consider the Medici family. Their banking dynasty, which stretched across Europe, did not grow by clinging to patriarchal control but by institutionalising it. The Medicis diversified ownership among family branches, trained successors relentlessly, and embedded governance rules that balanced authority with accountability. Even when individual members faltered, the structure endured long enough to reshape the economic map of Europe. Their power waned only when the structural rigour eroded, a reminder that foresight is not a one-off decision but a discipline to be maintained.

Nor were the Medicis alone. The Hanseatic League, a federation of merchant guilds in northern Europe, survived for centuries not because any one trader was irreplaceable but because systems outlived individuals. Merchants pooled resources, created enforceable contracts, and rotated leadership. They built what we would now call a *transferable enterprise*—designed for succession, not eternal personal rule. Their example reminds us that continuity depends less on charisma and more on architecture.

Fast forward to the nineteenth century. As industrial capitalism expanded, so too did the art of succession planning. Alfred Krupp, the German steel magnate, wrote a will in 1873 that did more than distribute wealth. It institutionalised the company's ownership in a foundation, ensuring that his successors would manage rather than liquidate the firm. This foresight secured the company's survival long after his death, creating one of Europe's most enduring industrial dynasties. Krupp's decision to embed his enterprise in legal scaffolding was not sentimental; it was strategic. He recognised that individual mortality is inevitable, but corporate mortality is optional.

Contrast this with contemporaries who ignored the principle. Countless Victorian manufacturers collapsed after the deaths of their founders because no mechanisms existed for continuity. Factories shuttered, employees dispersed, and innovations died with their inventors. History rarely records these failures; they vanish from the archive as completely as they did from the market. Yet their silence speaks loudly: enterprises without foresight do not endure.

In the modern age, the lesson persists. Japanese *keiretsu* and family firms embody centuries of cultural commitment to succession. Many family-owned *ryokan* inns or sake breweries still operating today have done so not through mythic founders but through institutionalised adoption, where capable heirs were brought into the family to ensure continuity. The practice may seem alien to Western readers, but its logic is universal: survival depends on prioritising structure over sentiment. Legacy is safeguarded not by clinging but by planning for release.

Contemporary conglomerates reveal similar wisdom. The Tata Group in India is not a one-man empire but a carefully governed network of companies managed by professional executives under the stewardship of trusts. This design has allowed it to thrive for over 150 years, weathering political upheaval and global shocks. Likewise, Samsung in South Korea, though often associated with powerful patriarchs, has invested heavily in succession systems that enable continuity through generational shifts. These institutions are not merely profitable; they embody a philosophy that ownership is temporary but stewardship must be permanent.

What unites these examples—from Renaissance bankers to Asian conglomerates—is a recognition of impermanence. Founders knew, either by philosophy or necessity, that no individual could anchor an enterprise forever. They understood mortality not as a threat but as a design parameter. Their foresight was not a denial of ambition but an extension of it: a determination to create something that would thrive beyond the self.

Modern entrepreneurs often resist this lesson. In a culture that idolises the visionary founder, we glorify the idea of eternal possession. But history teaches otherwise. Continuity does not depend on heroic control but on systems that make leadership replaceable. The merchants of Florence, the steel magnates of Germany, the conglomerates of Asia—they all understood that foresight was not optional. It was survival.

And so the question lingers: why, in a world more volatile than theirs, do so many founders still build as though succession were an afterthought? History has already given its verdict. The only enterprises that endure are those designed to outlast the hands that first shaped them.

The Cost of Ignoring the End

When Howard Schultz returned to Starbucks in 2008, the company was not bankrupt, but it was drifting dangerously close to irrelevance. Stores had multiplied beyond reason, quality had declined, and the once-revered brand was losing its magic. What saved Starbucks was not luck but a founder stepping back in because no succession plan had been properly embedded. The company recovered, but the episode revealed a precarious truth: even successful businesses stumble when leadership succession is treated as optional. For every Starbucks that manages a revival, there are dozens of quieter stories where businesses never recover—where the absence of a plan for the end ensures the end comes prematurely.

The ruins of these failures are everywhere, though they often fade quickly from public memory. Consider Pan American World Airways. Once the most glamorous airline in the world, "Pan Am" symbolised the jet age, pioneering routes and innovations that reshaped travel. Yet the company was so closely identified with founder Juan Trippe's leadership style that, after his departure, it floundered. There was no institutional succession plan robust enough to sustain the business. A series of reactive decisions followed—ill-considered acquisitions, patchwork leadership changes, and mounting debts—until the company finally collapsed in 1991. What was lost was more than an airline. It was an institution that had once defined modern aviation.

Family businesses, too, often fall victim to the refusal to imagine succession. Studies consistently show that fewer than one-third of family firms survive into the second generation, and fewer than one in ten reach the third.

Behind these statistics are stories of siblings embroiled in lawsuits, of children inheriting companies they neither understand nor want, and of loyal employees left adrift when owners die without clear transition plans. One well-known example is New York's Goudy's, a century-old department store that dissolved in the late twentieth century when heirs could not agree on leadership. The business was profitable; what killed it was the absence of foresight.

The emotional devastation is no less real than the financial. Founders who fail to plan often leave behind not just wreckage but guilt. Employees feel abandoned, communities lose a source of stability, and families fracture under the strain of contested inheritances. What might have been a proud legacy curdles into bitterness. In some cases, the very reputation of the founder is tarnished by their refusal to let go. The enterprise dies with them, and their name becomes a cautionary tale rather than a badge of honour.

Why does this happen so frequently, despite abundant evidence of the risks? The psychology is deceptively simple. To plan an exit is to acknowledge mortality, fallibility, and impermanence. Many founders resist until illness or crisis forces the issue. By then, it is too late to design continuity; desperation shapes the outcome instead. The irony is cruel: in trying to avoid the pain of confronting the end, leaders create far greater pain for everyone else.

There is also a philosophical dimension. Businesses that ignore succession implicitly treat ownership as personal possession rather than stewardship. The enterprise becomes an extension of ego rather than a shared institution. When that ego falters, so too does the business. By contrast, history shows that enterprises designed with succession in mind—from Renaissance banks to modern conglomerates—treat the business not as the founder's property but as a structure entrusted to them temporarily. The distinction between possession and stewardship is not semantic; it determines survival.

Modern case studies abound. Technology start-ups often burn brightly and fade quickly when founders fail to design for replacement. WeWork's implosion under Adam Neumann offers a vivid reminder of what happens when a charismatic leader refuses to imagine life beyond their control. Investors were left scrambling, employees disillusioned, and the company's once-promising valuation decimated. The collapse was not merely financial; it was psychological, the product of a culture shaped entirely around a single personality with no exit plan in sight.

These failures underscore a hard truth: refusing to imagine the end does not prevent it. It merely ensures it arrives unplanned, often in the worst possible form. A death without a will, a resignation without a successor, a sale forced under duress—these are the legacies of founders who mistake permanence for loyalty. Their enterprises pay the price, but so too do the people who depended on them.

And so a question lingers uncomfortably: what is the greater betrayal—to sell too soon, or to cling too long? The evidence from history and modern commerce suggests the latter. Yet still, many founders convince themselves that defiance of the end is a mark of devotion. Until that myth is dismantled, the cost of ignoring the end will continue to be measured in ruined enterprises, fractured communities, and legacies cut short. The reckoning always comes—whether planned or imposed. The only choice is whether it arrives as continuity or collapse.

Chapter 2
Defining Value Beyond Profit

In 2014, a promising start-up in the logistics sector turned down a lucrative acquisition offer. The founders, convinced their rising revenues would continue to justify ever-higher valuations, scoffed at what they saw as a lowball bid. Three years later, the company collapsed under the weight of operational chaos, leaving investors embittered and employees jobless. What had seemed like growth was, in truth, a fragile façade: systems had not kept pace with expansion, customer trust was eroding, and no buyer would touch the wreckage. Revenue had blinded the founders to the deeper question: what is a business actually worth when ownership changes hands?

The episode captures a paradox at the heart of entrepreneurship. Founders often equate value with profit: how much money the business generates and how quickly revenues are climbing. Buyers, by contrast, look through a different lens. They are less seduced by the top line than by what lies beneath it—predictability of earnings, risk exposure, and the ease with which the enterprise can be transferred. A founder may see record sales as proof of triumph; an investor may see an unscalable system, a fragile culture, or a volatile customer base as signs of fragility. The divergence is stark, and misunderstanding it is fatal to exit planning.

This divergence is not new. In the nineteenth century, bankers financing railroads were far less interested in how many passengers travelled on a given day than in whether the company could maintain its lines, manage its debts, and protect itself from competitors. They understood that *continuity*, not immediate profit, was the true currency of value. The principle has only sharpened in the modern age. Whether one examines the acquisition of Instagram by Facebook or the collapse of WeWork's IPO, the lesson is the same: cash flow is only part of the equation. Buyers purchase durability, not drama.

At its core, this chapter addresses a shift in perspective. Value, from the standpoint of a buyer, is not measured in how dazzling a founder appears in a pitch or how steep the revenue curve looks on a slide deck. It is measured in transferability. Can the company thrive without its creator at the centre? Are its systems resilient enough to scale, its brand strong enough to retain loyalty, its culture coherent enough to survive transition? Buyers are not purchasing stories; they are purchasing assets capable of withstanding the shock of change.

This is why the question of *what buyers really buy* is so critical. At the negotiation table, the conversation may orbit around cash flow multiples and projected growth, but the hidden calculus involves subtler elements: a well-documented operations manual, a loyal customer base, a reputation for integrity, or a team that functions independently of the founder. These elements rarely appear in glossy revenue reports, yet they often tip the balance of valuation. A company with modest profits but bulletproof systems may fetch more than a faster-growing competitor plagued by instability.

Invisible factors matter too—perhaps more than ever in a world where information flows quickly and reputations can collapse overnight. Culture, trust, and credibility cannot be neatly quantified, yet buyers know their absence can poison an acquisition. The scandal-ridden company, no matter how profitable, risks contaminating the buyer's own brand. Conversely, firms with reputations for ethical conduct, transparent governance, and healthy internal cultures become magnets for suitors. In this sense, a founder's daily decisions about how to treat employees, suppliers, and customers quietly accumulate into something priceless: reputational capital.

Yet there is another, more counterintuitive dimension. Growth, if pursued recklessly, can reduce value. This is a truth founders often resist. Expansion is celebrated in entrepreneurial culture as a sign of vigour; headlines trumpet record-breaking scaling. But when growth outruns infrastructure, when customer service lags, when financial controls buckle, value erodes. Buyers see not a success story but a liability. To them, "more" can mean "less"—a swelling revenue base accompanied by rising risk, dissatisfied customers, and strained systems. Such businesses may dazzle from a distance yet repel scrutiny during due diligence.

This reality forces a deeper philosophical reflection. Is value located in the excitement of growth or in the stability of continuity? Founders intoxicated by momentum often answer the former; buyers, tasked with safeguarding capital, insist on the latter. The tension between these perspectives is not easily reconciled, but recognising it is essential. Only by bridging the founder's lens and the investor's lens can a business be prepared for a successful exit.

The stakes are immense. Misunderstanding value can mean the difference between a lucrative sale and a wasted legacy, between continuity and collapse. This chapter invites readers to rethink their assumptions, to see beyond revenue and growth charts, and to interrogate the less visible elements that determine worth. Systems, brands, cultures, reputations—these are not peripheral concerns but central pillars of valuation.

And the unresolved question remains: if value is more than profit, how should founders act differently today, while still in control, to create a business that others will one day want to own? The answer lies ahead, in the shift from thinking like an operator to thinking like a steward of transferable assets. Only then does profit become not the destination but the evidence of something deeper: durability.

The Investor's Lens vs. the Founder's Lens

In 2019, a European technology start-up boasting impressive year-on-year revenue growth was preparing for a major funding round. Its founders were convinced the business was worth ten times its annual sales. When investors entered due diligence, however, their verdict was sobering: systems were patchy, contracts were informal, and the company's reliance on one charismatic founder was acute. For the entrepreneurs, the company looked like a rocket ship ready to soar. For the investors, it looked like an aircraft without landing gear. The valuation gap was not the product of malice but of perspective—two radically different ways of seeing the same enterprise.

This dissonance between founder and investor is at the heart of exit planning. Founders often measure value in emotional terms: years of sweat equity, the symbolic importance of their creation, the recognition earned through growth. Even when they use financial metrics, they are prone to celebrate the topline—revenues, customer counts, market buzz. Investors, by contrast, are trained to distrust glamour. Their gaze cuts deeper, to questions of predictability, durability, and risk. They know that a business's worth is not what it generates under one leader, but what it can reliably produce under another.

The contrast can feel jarring. Founders speak in stories; investors speak in probabilities. One frames value as proof of vision, the other as insurance against collapse. Neither is wrong, but unless the two are reconciled, negotiations stumble and opportunities evaporate.

At the centre of the investor's lens lies *predictability*. A business that generates £10 million one year and £3 million the next may, to its founder, look like an exciting but turbulent growth narrative. To an investor, it looks like a dangerous gamble. Predictability of earnings—not their occasional brilliance—is what commands higher multiples. Subscription models, recurring contracts, sticky customer relationships: these are the features that transform businesses into reliable machines rather than speculative bets. A founder may find such regularity dull; an investor finds it beautiful.

Closely tied to predictability is *risk*. Founders are accustomed to living with risk. They normalise volatility, improvising constantly, surviving by force of will. But investors seek precisely the opposite. They look for evidence that risk has been managed, distributed, or engineered away. A company reliant on a single supplier, a handful of customers, or one key executive is, to them, a fragile construct waiting to collapse. Reducing such concentrations is not peripheral housekeeping—it is central to value.

Then comes *growth potential*, perhaps the most seductive of all measures. Founders often emphasise growth rates as a badge of success. But investors probe the quality of that growth. Is it profitable or subsidised by endless capital injections? Is it sustainable or fuelled by unsustainable discounts? Growth that strains systems, alienates customers, or burns staff may inflate short-term revenue while corroding long-term worth. To investors, such expansion is not impressive; it is alarming.

Case studies illuminate the gulf. When Facebook acquired Instagram in 2012 for $1 billion, many scoffed at the price tag for a company with no revenue. Yet investors saw something founders often underestimate: transferability of value. Instagram had an engaged user base, scalable technology, and cultural momentum that could outlast its small founding team. By contrast, consider WeWork's disastrous attempt to go public in 2019. Its founders pointed to meteoric revenue growth; investors saw uncontrolled risk, an opaque business model, and dependence on a mercurial leader. The implosion wiped out tens of billions in paper value, a stark reminder that glamour without governance is worthless.

Philosophically, the tension between lenses reflects two different relationships to time. Founders live in the present: solving today's problems, chasing today's opportunities, convincing themselves that their intensity can sustain tomorrow. Investors live in the future: discounting risks, modelling scenarios, asking not "what is this worth now?" but "what will it yield, predictably, in five years?" The founder's lens is autobiographical; the investor's is actuarial. Both have merit, but only the latter sets the terms of acquisition.

The implications for founders are profound. To bridge the gap, they must learn to see themselves as outsiders would. That means treating their company not as a reflection of identity but as a portfolio of assets. Which revenues are repeatable? Which systems are independent of personality?

Which risks have been neutralised, and which lurk unseen? It requires a humility that can feel unnatural, a willingness to admit that passion is not value, and charisma is not continuity.

The divergence between founder and investor lenses is not a flaw in the system but a structural reality. It forces entrepreneurs to confront uncomfortable truths about what they have built. It also offers a chance for transformation. By adopting the investor's gaze, even temporarily, founders can anticipate objections, shore up weaknesses, and build companies that survive scrutiny. They can learn that the true test of value is not how brightly the enterprise shines in their own eyes, but how durable it appears when stripped of their presence.

Yet a lingering tension remains. If investors prize predictability, are we in danger of stifling the very risk-taking that fuels innovation? Might the investor's lens undervalue boldness, just as the founder's lens overvalues it? The question has no simple answer. But it is precisely in wrestling with that ambiguity that entrepreneurs can begin to design businesses that are both visionary and viable—worthy of their passion, and attractive to those who must one day take the reins.

What Buyers Really Buy

In 2009, when Kraft Foods acquired Cadbury for £11.5 billion, critics were quick to question the price. Analysts pointed to profit margins, debt structures, and commodity costs. But Kraft was not simply buying chocolate bars; it was acquiring a brand with more than a century of cultural trust, distribution systems that reached into the farthest corners of the world, and a loyal customer base spanning generations. What Kraft purchased was not only cash flow but *transferable assets*: the machinery of continuity, the infrastructure of trust, the systems and relationships that would endure long after the ink on the contracts dried.

This paradox—between what appears to be bought and what is truly bought—lies at the heart of most acquisitions. Founders, deeply invested in the day-to-day grind, often imagine that buyers are paying for revenue, profits, or growth rates. But these are only the surface indicators. Beneath them lies the true object of the transaction: the *durability* of the business without its founder. What buyers are actually purchasing is freedom from uncertainty. They pay for processes that can replicate success, for brands that command loyalty, and for customers who will remain when leadership changes hands.

To miss this truth is to misread the market. A founder dazzled by their own top-line growth may find their company dismissed as unsellable if systems are ad hoc, reputations fragile, or customers fickle. Conversely, a firm with modest profits but impeccable processes and a strong cultural identity can command a premium far beyond what spreadsheets predict.

Systems as Value

Buyers prize systems because systems reduce dependency. A restaurant dependent on the founder's charisma may fill tables while they are present, but the moment they step away, demand falters. By contrast, a chain with replicable recipes, training manuals, and disciplined operations can thrive in dozens of cities simultaneously. McDonald's is the archetype: what buyers invest in is not burgers but a finely tuned system of processes, franchising models, and real estate strategies that scale predictably.

This is why due diligence scrutinises not only financials but also procedures: supply chain contracts, documentation of workflows, customer service protocols. The question is always the same: can this business operate without its founder? If the answer is no, value evaporates. Systems are the silent assets that investors prize most, even if founders underestimate them.

Brands as Value

Equally critical is the brand—the intangible promise that resides in the minds of customers. Brands are not simply logos or advertising campaigns; they are reservoirs of trust. When Coca-Cola's name appears on a bottle, consumers expect consistency, and buyers know that expectation translates into reliable revenue. This explains why companies often fetch valuations far exceeding their tangible assets. Google's search algorithms, Nike's swoosh, Apple's bitten apple: these symbols carry gravitational pull.

For founders, brand-building may feel like a side effect of growth; for buyers, it is often the core attraction. A brand that commands loyalty cushions against competition, stabilises demand, and provides pricing power. It is no accident that in many acquisitions, from Unilever's purchase of Dollar Shave Club to L'Oréal's acquisition of smaller beauty start-ups, the premium reflects not factories or sales figures but the resonance of the brand with consumers.

Customers as Value

The third pillar is the customer base. Investors do not simply buy current sales; they buy relationships. A loyal, diverse, and engaged customer base reduces risk and increases predictability. By contrast, a company reliant on a handful of clients, however lucrative, represents fragility. A single defection could topple the business.

This is why subscription models and recurring revenue streams command such admiration in modern markets. Buyers love predictability, and nothing is more predictable than customers who return month after month by default. Salesforce, Spotify, and Netflix are valued not just for growth but for the stability of subscription-driven relationships. For founders, this should be a reminder: cultivating enduring customer ties is as critical as boosting quarterly revenues.

Yet there is a subtler dimension to what buyers truly purchase: the invisible glue that binds systems, brands, and customers together. A company may have strong processes, a recognisable brand, and a broad customer base, but if its culture is toxic or its reputation tainted, the value is brittle. Consider Uber in its early years. Its growth was spectacular, its customer base global, yet its toxic internal culture and reputational scandals nearly derailed its IPO. Buyers recognised that culture is not cosmetic—it shapes everything from employee retention to brand perception.

The lesson is clear. What is acquired is not the business as it looks today but its *capacity to endure tomorrow*. Systems, brands, and customers are the pillars of that endurance. Without them, cash flow is ephemeral. With them, even modest enterprises can become enduring institutions.

The implication for founders is unsettling. They must learn to see their businesses as outsiders do—not as passion projects or reflections of self, but as bundles of transferable assets. This requires detachment, discipline, and an almost architectural perspective: designing each element not merely for today's use but for tomorrow's handover.

The unresolved tension remains: in building for transferability, do founders risk hollowing out the very passion that gave the business life? Or might the act of systematising, brand-building, and cultivating customers actually protect passion from burnout? Buyers know the answer instinctively. They do not buy passion itself; they buy its translation into durable structures. The question for founders is whether they are willing to make that translation—or whether they will remain trapped in a business valuable only while they remain at its centre.

Invisible Value: Culture and Reputation

In 2001, when Enron imploded almost overnight, it was not because the company lacked assets, infrastructure, or a customer base. On paper, Enron was a powerhouse; in practice, its culture of deception and its shredded reputation rendered it worthless the moment the truth surfaced. Investors, customers, and employees fled, and what had been one of the largest companies in the United States collapsed into bankruptcy in weeks. The lesson endures: culture and reputation—those intangible qualities often dismissed as "soft"—can be the ultimate determinants of value.

At the other end of the spectrum stands Patagonia. When Yvon Chouinard announced in 2022 that he was giving away ownership of the company to a trust and a non-profit dedicated to fighting climate change, the response was overwhelmingly positive. Customers flocked to celebrate, employees swelled with pride, and the brand's reputation for integrity deepened. Patagonia's products did not suddenly become technically superior overnight; what increased its value was an intangible—an alignment of culture, values, and reputation that amplified trust.

Buyers understand this acutely. They know that numbers on a balance sheet are vulnerable to erosion, but a strong culture and a trusted reputation can sustain value through crises, leadership transitions, and shifting markets. These factors rarely appear directly in financial reports, yet they can make or break a deal. Indeed, private equity firms frequently cite cultural fit and reputational stability as critical variables in acquisition decisions. They are not paying merely for profits; they are paying for confidence that the enterprise will endure without hidden rot.

Culture is the invisible architecture of a business. It shapes how employees behave when no one is watching, how decisions are made under pressure, and whether innovation thrives or suffocates. A toxic culture can corrode even the most impressive revenues. Uber's early growth revealed this: while customers adopted the service at a blistering pace, its culture of aggression, misconduct, and disregard for governance sparked scandals that nearly derailed the company's public offering. Investors were forced to weigh not only financial upside but also reputational risk—a calculation that tempered enthusiasm and lowered valuation.

By contrast, companies with coherent, positive cultures often outperform in ways that seem disproportionate to their size. Take Trader Joe's, the American grocery chain. Its financial model is unremarkable compared with larger competitors, yet its quirky, employee-friendly culture translates into fierce customer loyalty and enviable profitability. Buyers and investors prize such businesses because culture, though intangible, manifests as resilience:

lower staff turnover, better customer service, and more consistent execution.

Reputation, meanwhile, functions as a form of social capital. It is the currency of trust exchanged with customers, suppliers, regulators, and communities. Once damaged, it is excruciatingly difficult to restore. Volkswagen's emissions scandal cost the company billions not only in fines but in long-term trust, weakening its brand across markets. For potential acquirers, reputational damage is a liability that lingers well beyond the immediate crisis. No buyer wants to inherit a poisoned brand, however attractive the financials may look.

There is also a deeper philosophical dimension. Culture and reputation speak to questions of character, both individual and collective. A founder may view their company's culture as an extension of personal values; buyers, however, are interested in whether those values can be institutionalised. Can the culture outlive the founder's presence? Will employees act with integrity when ownership changes? If the answer is no, then what appears valuable is fragile. Reputation, similarly, is a mirror held up to the outside world. It reflects how well the company has honoured its promises—not just in marketing campaigns, but in lived relationships.

Protecting and enhancing these intangible assets demands discipline. For culture, this means codifying values into hiring practices, performance incentives, and governance structures. For reputation, it means radical transparency, ethical conduct, and consistent delivery on promises. It is not enough to *say* the right things; buyers look for evidence that the business has woven these values into its daily operations. Corporate governance, whistleblower policies, employee engagement surveys—all are signals that culture and reputation are actively cultivated, not left to chance.

The paradox is that these intangibles are often neglected precisely because they do not appear on traditional financial statements. Founders can be so focused on revenues and margins that they fail to notice cultural decay or reputational cracks until it is too late. Yet when buyers evaluate opportunities, they instinctively privilege these intangibles. Numbers can be massaged; reputation cannot. Systems can be rebuilt; trust, once squandered, may never return.

For founders preparing to exit, the challenge is both practical and existential. How do you demonstrate to an outsider that your company's culture is healthy and your reputation strong? The answer lies less in rhetoric than in proof: low turnover, high employee satisfaction, transparent governance, and a public record unmarred by scandal. Just as importantly, founders must recognise that culture and reputation are not ornaments but engines of value.

And yet, a question lingers uncomfortably: can these intangible assets truly be preserved once a business changes hands? Does culture survive new ownership, or is it inevitably reshaped? Can a reputation built over decades be transferred intact, or does it risk dilution? Buyers may believe they are acquiring stability, but perhaps they are acquiring something far more fragile—a trust that can never be fully commodified. The answer to this tension will determine not only the price of the deal but the legacy of the enterprise itself.

When Growth Reduces Value

In 2019, WeWork was preparing for what was supposed to be one of the most anticipated IPOs of the decade. Revenues had grown at a dizzying pace, global offices multiplied in the hundreds, and headlines lauded its disruption of the commercial real estate market. Yet when investors finally looked under the hood, they recoiled. Losses ballooned, governance was chaotic, systems were immature, and the company's dependence on endless capital injections was unsustainable. Growth, rather than adding value, had stripped it away. In the end, the IPO collapsed, billions in valuation evaporated, and the company became a cautionary tale: expansion without discipline is not strength but fragility.

This paradox unsettles the very mythology of entrepreneurship. Growth is celebrated as the ultimate measure of success: more customers, more markets, more revenue. Yet in the world of acquisitions, *more* can mean *less*. Rapid scaling, if unmanaged, exposes weaknesses instead of concealing them. It magnifies cracks in systems, stretches culture to breaking point, and attracts scrutiny from buyers who see risk where founders see triumph. What appears to the entrepreneur as momentum can appear to the investor as a liability in disguise.

The logic is deceptively simple. Growth demands infrastructure—systems, processes, leadership capacity—that must evolve in lockstep with revenue. When they do not, instability accumulates. Consider the story of Groupon. Lauded as the fastest-growing company in history, it expanded into dozens of countries within a few years. But its model was easily replicable, its merchant relationships strained, and its customer loyalty shallow. By the time it went public in 2011, investors saw not a revolutionary company but a fragile construct with no path to sustained profitability. The stock collapsed, and much of the value once promised evaporated.

Growth can also corrode culture, another silent but critical determinant of value. Start-ups often thrive in early stages on shared vision and informal camaraderie. Yet when headcount doubles or triples in short bursts, cohesion frays. Communication falters, decision-making slows, and the clarity of purpose that once defined the company dissipates. Buyers are not blind to this. They understand that a fragmented culture weakens execution and undermines reputation. Scaling too fast without preserving coherence can turn an energetic team into a disjointed workforce—and in the eyes of acquirers, that translates into risk.

There is also the issue of financial optics. Growth often requires debt, aggressive discounting, or costly customer acquisition campaigns. While these may inflate revenues in the short term, they erode margins and create dependency on unsustainable strategies. Buyers, who look for durable earnings rather than vanity metrics, discount such growth heavily. They know that a business addicted to subsidies is not a business built to last.

The counterintuitive reality is that slower, disciplined growth can create more exit value than rapid, chaotic expansion. Investors prize predictability over spectacle. A company that grows at 20 per cent annually with solid margins, robust systems, and a loyal customer base is often valued more highly than one growing at 80 per cent but haemorrhaging cash and struggling to maintain order. It is not velocity that counts but quality—the assurance that growth will persist after the founder exits.

The philosophical tension runs deep. Growth appeals to ego: it signals ambition, dominance, conquest. It flatters the founder's identity as a visionary who can bend markets to their will. But investors are less impressed by ego than by endurance. To them, the true test of leadership is restraint—the willingness to expand only as quickly as systems, people, and culture can bear. In this light, value lies not in how big a business becomes but in how well it preserves integrity as it grows.

The challenge, of course, is psychological. Founders are under constant pressure—from markets, from media, from peers—to equate size with worth. To slow down feels like weakness, even betrayal of ambition. Yet the irony is that restraint often yields a higher eventual payoff. Buyers reward those who resist the seduction of reckless scaling because they know such discipline signals maturity, foresight, and sustainability.

Case studies abound. Amazon scaled relentlessly but with obsessive attention to systems and infrastructure, reinvesting profits into logistics, technology, and customer experience. Its growth created value because it was undergirded by discipline. By contrast, companies like Pets.com or Quibi expanded noisily, chasing audiences and market share without the ballast of sustainable economics. Their collapses remind us that growth pursued for its own sake is indistinguishable from speculation.

The uncomfortable truth is that not all growth is good. Some growth is cancerous: it spreads rapidly, consumes resources, and weakens the host. The task for founders is to distinguish between growth that compounds value and growth that destroys it. That requires humility, patience, and the courage to design systems as carefully as they chase sales.

And so a provocative question lingers: if more can mean less, what does it mean to grow well? The answer lies not in the headline figures of revenue or reach, but in the quieter metrics of durability—customer loyalty, cultural strength, operational resilience. These are the forms of growth that survive scrutiny, survive succession, and survive time itself. The rest may glitter for a season, but when buyers arrive, the shine fades, and what once looked like triumph is revealed as fragility in disguise.

Chapter 3
Systems as the Silent Valuator

In 1997, when Ray Kroc's heirs sold McDonald's shares to institutional investors, the golden arches did not waver. The founders had long been absent, the original hamburgers of the 1950s a distant memory, yet the company's value did not lie in personalities or nostalgia. It lay in the system—an intricate choreography of supply chains, franchising rules, staff training, and brand consistency—that ensured every Big Mac tasted the same in Chicago, Tokyo, or Johannesburg. McDonald's was not sold as a restaurant chain but as a replicable process. The systems were the product, and that was precisely what made it transferable at scale.

Contrast that with the countless small businesses that thrive while their founders are present but evaporate when they leave. The corner café where customers come for the owner's smile, the consultancy that relies on a charismatic leader's contacts, the start-up driven entirely by the technical brilliance of one coder—such enterprises may appear healthy, but they are unsellable. The absence of systems renders them fragile, and buyers know it. Without process, a business is not a business but a personality project, and personality cannot be transferred.

This chapter examines the silent determinant of valuation: systems. Founders often underestimate their importance, mistaking improvisation for agility and personal oversight for quality control. But investors see through such illusions. What they look for is predictability, efficiency, and resilience—qualities that can only be embedded in systems, not individuals. Systems may lack glamour, but they are the infrastructure of trust in a transaction. They signal that the enterprise is designed to endure transitions, not collapse under them.

The logic is straightforward but profound. A company with robust systems demonstrates that knowledge has been codified, risks mitigated, and operations made replicable. This reduces dependency on individuals and turns unpredictable human behaviour into reliable outcomes. When Amazon scales globally, it is not because Jeff Bezos personally oversees deliveries but because processes—from fulfilment centres to recommendation algorithms—operate with precision. Technology amplifies this, acting as the backbone that allows processes to be standardised, monitored, and improved. Buyers value such systems not as add-ons but as proof of durability.

The implications extend beyond logistics. Customer service, decision-making frameworks, financial reporting—all can either be ad hoc and founder-dependent or systematised and transferable. Buyers scrutinise these areas during due diligence with a checklist mentality: are records clear, workflows documented, compliance secured? A missing system is not a minor oversight; it is a red flag that lowers valuation or kills the deal outright. Conversely, businesses that present polished systems create confidence, accelerating negotiations and increasing multiples.

There is also a philosophical dimension. Systems represent a shift from founder-centric identity to institutional identity. They are the bridge between passion and permanence, transforming vision into structure. For many entrepreneurs, this transition is uncomfortable. It requires ceding control, documenting instincts, and acknowledging that personal brilliance is not scalable. Yet it is precisely this surrender that converts a fragile enterprise into an enduring one.

And here lies the paradox worth dwelling on: the more a founder embeds themselves into every decision, the less valuable their business becomes. The more they replace themselves with processes, the more transferable—and thus more valuable—the enterprise is. Buyers are not seeking to purchase a person's energy; they are seeking to purchase the assurance that, once that person steps away, the machinery continues to turn.

This chapter explores how to make that paradox work in your favour. It will show why replacing the founder with process is the first act of creating true value, how scalable systems form the backbone of consistency, how technology elevates transferability, and why investors arrive armed with checklists that test the solidity of what you have built.

The question it poses is stark but liberating: will your company survive without you? If the answer is yes, its value grows. If the answer is no, then no amount of revenue will compensate. Systems are the hidden currency of continuity, and for those who master them, they become the silent but decisive factor in turning a business into a sellable, enduring asset.

Replacing the Founder With Process

In 2012, the sudden death of Fausto Dotti, a celebrated Italian restaurateur, sent shockwaves through his community. His flagship trattoria, revered by critics and locals alike, closed its doors within six months. It wasn't for lack of loyal customers or strong revenue. The tragedy was structural: every recipe, every supplier relationship, every decision lived in Fausto's head. Without him, there was no system—only a void. What had seemed like a thriving enterprise was, in truth, a fragile extension of one man's charisma. The collapse was not the result of poor business acumen, but of dependence on personality where process should have been.

This is the paradox at the heart of founder-led businesses: the very qualities that ignite their growth can later threaten their survival. Founders often pour themselves so completely into their companies that the line between self and enterprise dissolves. Their instincts shape strategy, their contacts fuel revenue, their reputation reassures clients. Yet this intimacy, once an asset, becomes a liability when succession or sale is contemplated. Buyers are not purchasing a person's energy; they are purchasing the promise of continuity. Where continuity rests on one individual, the business becomes unsellable.

The most enduring companies in history have recognised this truth. Henry Ford was a visionary, but Ford Motor Company did not thrive for a century because of his presence; it thrived because of the assembly line. That invention was more than an industrial breakthrough—it was the codification of knowledge into process. The genius of the founder was embedded into the machinery, so the enterprise could endure beyond his lifetime. The lesson is stark: if a business is to outlive its founder, the founder must render themselves dispensable.

Replacing personality with process begins with acknowledging a psychological barrier. Many entrepreneurs find it difficult to let go because their authority is tied to their indispensability. The founder as bottleneck feels powerful, even flattering—every decision sought, every crisis resolved at their desk. But this dynamic suffocates scalability. A company reliant on a single brain is inherently capped, its value anchored to mortality and availability. Documenting processes, training others, and delegating authority feels, at first, like dilution. In fact, it is multiplication—the conversion of individual expertise into institutional memory.

Modern case studies abound. Consider Howard Schultz's tenure at Starbucks. For years, Schultz's personal involvement was seen as the company's lifeblood. But when he stepped aside in 2000, the company faltered precisely because so many systems—particularly those related to brand consistency and customer experience—depended on his direct guidance. Only when Starbucks institutionalised its operating principles, from supply chain to store design, did it become truly resilient. The resurgence of the company was less about Schultz's return and more about the systems that allowed Starbucks to deliver the same experience in Seoul as in Seattle.

Systems also protect against the idiosyncrasies of founder leadership. Charismatic founders may excel in winning clients but falter in compliance. Brilliant product designers may innovate ceaselessly but neglect financial discipline. By embedding standards into systems—checklists, software protocols, training manuals—companies convert personal strengths into organisational assets while mitigating personal weaknesses. Investors look for this balance: not how brilliant the founder is, but how little the business depends on that brilliance.

The philosophical stakes are significant. Replacing oneself with process is not an act of abdication but of legacy. It is the moment when vision transcends personality. In ancient guilds, master craftsmen created apprenticeships not only to pass on skills but to ensure their craft endured beyond their own hands. The same principle applies in modern enterprise. Codifying methods, designing replicable operations, and empowering successors is the ultimate act of stewardship. The founder ceases to be the business and instead becomes its architect, enabling the structure to stand independent of them.

Yet this transition is rarely smooth. Resistance comes not only from the founder but from employees conditioned to rely on their presence. Clients too may need reassurance that quality does not evaporate with the individual. Here, transparent communication and gradual systematisation matter. The founder must show that the company is bigger than any one person, that excellence has been embedded in processes, not left floating in personality. The most successful transitions are those that happen quietly, when customers scarcely notice the founder's absence because the experience remains seamless.

What, then, does replacing the founder with process require in practice? It demands rigorous documentation of routines and decision frameworks, from onboarding staff to handling client complaints. It requires investing in training so knowledge is dispersed, not hoarded. It insists on establishing governance structures—clear roles, accountability mechanisms, and reporting systems—that do not collapse when one chair is empty. It calls for technology that standardises and scales, whether through customer relationship management systems, financial dashboards, or workflow automation.

But beneath the mechanics lies an existential question: is the founder willing to let go? To trade indispensability for scalability? To accept that their greatest contribution may not be their constant presence but their deliberate absence, made possible by the systems they leave behind? It is a difficult but liberating shift, one that transforms a company from a personal achievement into a transferable asset.

The companies that master this are the ones buyers covet. They are enterprises where the founder's spirit lingers in the design but not in the day-to-day execution. They are organisations that function as smoothly in the founder's absence as in their presence. And for every founder who dreams of freedom—whether through sale, succession, or simply stepping back—this is the indispensable step.

The haunting question remains: if you walked away tomorrow, would your business continue to run? For many founders, the honest answer is no. And until that answer changes, the company is not a company at all, but an extension of one person's will. True value, as investors well know, begins the moment process replaces personality.

Designing Scalable Systems

In 2008, an Icelandic bakery named Brauð & Co. became a small sensation in Reykjavik. Locals raved about its cinnamon buns, tourists queued outside the shop, and journalists hailed it as a hidden gem. But as the bakery's fame grew, cracks appeared. Each bun tasted slightly different depending on who was working the ovens that day. Customers returned expecting the flavour of their first bite, only to encounter inconsistency. Expansion plans faltered. What was missing was not talent or demand, but replicable systems. Without them, growth was a burden, not an opportunity.

This anecdote captures a universal truth: businesses do not scale on personality or luck. They scale on repeatability. A single artisan can produce excellence, but excellence multiplied across dozens of hands, across hundreds of locations, requires frameworks. It is here, in the careful design of operational, customer service, and decision-making systems, that true scalability resides. These systems are not glamorous; they lack the allure of innovation or branding. Yet, silently, they determine whether a business can expand without fracturing under its own weight.

The paradox is stark. Most founders dream of growth, but growth exposes the limits of improvisation. What works in a team of five collapses under the strain of fifty. What delights a dozen loyal clients may enrage hundreds if not delivered consistently. Growth, far from rewarding informality, punishes it. The businesses that endure are those that treat systems not as bureaucratic red tape, but as the scaffolding of freedom.

Designing scalable systems begins with operations—the machinery of how things get done. Consider McDonald's. Critics may deride its culinary value, but few companies have mastered operational scalability with such precision. From Tokyo to Toronto, the process of flipping a burger is identical, governed by scripts, timers, and checklists. This does not happen by chance; it is the product of relentless refinement. Investors understand this. A company that can guarantee output without the founder's oversight demonstrates transferability—the holy grail of valuation.

Customer service offers another illustration. Zappos, the American online shoe retailer, built its reputation on obsessive service quality. At first, this seemed an intangible: cheerful staff, long phone calls, spontaneous gestures of generosity. But behind the scenes, Zappos embedded systems—training protocols, cultural rituals, and incentive structures—that ensured the experience could scale. Kindness, codified, became part of the business model. Buyers are not just purchasing call centres; they are purchasing the system that ensures every interaction sustains the brand promise.

Decision-making, too, must be systematised if scale is to succeed. Many founders cling to centralised control, believing their judgement is irreplaceable. Yet a company cannot grow if every question must rise to the founder's desk. Scalable systems distribute authority without sacrificing coherence. This is why companies adopt frameworks like the RACI model (responsible, accountable, consulted, informed) or OKRs (objectives and key results). They are not corporate jargon for its own sake; they are decision-making scaffolds, designed to free organisations from bottlenecks and allow dozens of managers to act in concert.

The philosophy underpinning scalable systems is deceptively simple: consistency is a form of respect. It respects the customer, who deserves the same product or service each time. It respects employees, who need clarity to perform confidently. And it respects investors, who value predictability above personality. Systems embody a kind of humility, acknowledging that memory is fallible, that charisma is not replicable, and that excellence cannot depend on chance.

Yet systems do not mean rigidity. The best frameworks are living, adaptive, and designed for iteration. Toyota's famed production system demonstrates this balance. Standardised workflows ensure consistency, but embedded within them is the practice of *kaizen*—continuous improvement. Employees at every level are empowered to suggest refinements. This paradox—discipline with adaptability—is what gives systems longevity. Rigid structures crumble; flexible systems endure.

Technology now accelerates this imperative. Digital platforms allow processes to be embedded not only in manuals but in software. Customer relationship management tools, automated billing systems, workflow trackers: these are not optional luxuries but essential mechanisms for scalability. Investors view them as signals of maturity, proof that the business can sustain growth without the founder's heroic effort. In this sense, technology is less about efficiency than about trust—the trust that tomorrow's operations will look like today's, no matter who sits in the chair.

Still, the act of designing scalable systems forces a difficult reckoning. Founders must relinquish the illusion that their presence guarantees quality. They must resist the temptation to intervene ad hoc, undermining the very systems they hope to build. This is often the hardest cultural shift: moving from a mentality of "I can fix it" to one of "the system will fix it." The discipline is as much psychological as operational.

The irony, of course, is that systems designed for scalability ultimately liberate the founder. They free the entrepreneur from the tyranny of constant oversight, transforming the business into a self-sustaining organism. Without them, growth is chaos; with them, growth becomes continuity.

The question is not whether systems will be built, but who will build them: the founder, proactively, or the market, brutally, through failure. Investors already know the answer. They will not pay for potential wrapped in chaos. They will pay—and pay generously—for predictability, reliability, and the invisible architecture of order. The true test for any founder is whether their enterprise can pass that audit of continuity.

So the unresolved tension remains: if your business doubled tomorrow, would it still deliver the same experience? Or would it break under its own ambition? The answer reveals not just your readiness for growth, but your readiness for exit. The silent valuator of every enterprise is not charisma, nor even profit—it is the integrity of its systems.

Technology as the Backbone

In 2014, Dollar Shave Club, a start-up that disrupted the grooming industry with its witty marketing and subscription model, was acquired by Unilever for $1 billion. Analysts pored over its customer base and brand personality, but behind the scenes, the real prize was something less glamorous: a robust digital infrastructure. Dollar Shave Club had perfected subscription logistics, automated billing, data-driven personalisation, and seamless fulfilment. Unilever was not buying razors; it was buying the system that ensured razors appeared predictably on millions of doorsteps each month. The deal underscored a truth increasingly visible across industries: technology is not an accessory to valuation, it is its backbone.

This may sound counterintuitive. Many founders still imagine their enterprise's worth as residing in tangible goods, visible profits, or charismatic brands. Yet buyers—especially institutional investors—are increasingly captivated by the unseen architecture: the systems of software, automation, and digital platforms that guarantee transferability. A thriving company without digital foundations is fragile; a modest business with well-structured technological systems is infinitely scalable. The market knows the difference.

The paradox lies in invisibility. Customers rarely notice when a company's digital infrastructure works flawlessly, but investors always do. Clean data trails, automated workflows, and scalable platforms are the subtle signals of resilience. They mean that ownership can change hands without chaos, that growth does not depend on improvisation, and that knowledge is captured in systems rather than trapped in the founder's head. In essence, technology makes the promise of continuity credible.

Consider Shopify, the e-commerce platform that powers millions of independent retailers. To outsiders, its success may look like a story of market timing and user-friendly design. But to investors, Shopify's real genius lies in the extensibility of its platform: the APIs, plug-ins, and cloud infrastructure that allow even the smallest merchant to operate with enterprise-level efficiency. A founder selling handmade ceramics in Brighton can now manage inventory, process international payments, and analyse customer behaviour with the same sophistication as a multinational retailer. The platform reduces fragility and increases transferability—two attributes that translate directly into valuation.

Technology also changes the calculus of risk. A company with fragmented spreadsheets, manual approvals, and opaque records exposes buyers to uncertainty. By contrast, a business running on integrated enterprise software offers transparency and verifiability. When due diligence reveals structured, retrievable, and accurate data, investors relax. They know they are buying not just the promise of profits, but the assurance of control. This is why cloud-based accounting platforms, CRM systems, and enterprise resource planning tools have become not optional add-ons but prerequisites for serious valuation.

Automation carries this further. Take Ocado, the British online supermarket. Its valuation has long exceeded that of many traditional grocers, not because of its brand recognition, but because of its proprietary warehouse robotics and logistics software. The system is so advanced that Ocado now licenses its technology to grocers worldwide. In effect, Ocado shifted from being a retailer to being a technology company, commanding multiples far above those justified by grocery margins. The lesson is stark: when technology is the backbone, a business transcends its industry.

But the relationship between technology and value is not simply mechanical. It also has a philosophical dimension. A founder may see their digital systems as tedious overheads, but an investor sees them as the codification of wisdom. Each automated process is a captured decision; each database, a memory bank; each workflow, an embodiment of foresight. Technology becomes a company's institutional brain. The more complete and integrated that brain, the more confidently it can be transplanted to new ownership.

The tension lies in investment priorities. Many entrepreneurs prefer to pour capital into visible growth—hiring staff, marketing campaigns, product development—while skimping on back-end systems. It feels rational: customers reward new features, not well-structured CRMs. Yet when the time comes to sell, those neglected systems surface as liabilities. What looked like thrift reveals itself as fragility. Investors discount the business, calculating the cost of retrofitting discipline onto chaos. Thus, ironically, technology spending that once seemed like a drain on growth turns out to have been the very foundation of transferable value.

There are, of course, cautionary tales. WeWork, at its peak, was valued at $47 billion, largely on brand aura and aggressive expansion. Yet its technology infrastructure was underwhelming: booking systems clunky, data fragmented, operations overly reliant on manual oversight. When investors scrutinised the business, they found charisma, not codified systems. The crash in valuation that followed was not simply a matter of overhype but of underbuilt backbone. The company's promises were not supported by replicable, automated processes.

The implications stretch beyond valuation mechanics. Technology changes the very nature of what it means to "own" a business. In a traditional enterprise, ownership meant controlling people and premises. In a digitally mature business, ownership means controlling code, data, and platforms. This shift challenges founders to reconceptualise their role. They are not simply managers of staff but architects of systems. To neglect this role is to leave the enterprise vulnerable; to embrace it is to future-proof both the business and its eventual transfer.

So, the question becomes unavoidable: is your business's technology serving merely as a tool, or is it already functioning as a backbone? Buyers will ask. Investors will test. And if the systems are missing, they will assume fragility where the founder insists there is resilience.

This is the quiet drama of valuation in the digital age. Technology does not shout its importance. It hums in the background, invisible to customers, unglamorous to founders, but glaringly obvious to investors. Its presence reassures; its absence alarms. The paradox remains: the less visible it is day to day, the more it shapes the price when it matters most.

And so the tension lingers: what is the true worth of a company without a technological backbone? Or, more provocatively still, in a world where value increasingly flows through software and automation, can a business without digital infrastructure be considered a business at all?

The Investor's Checklist

In 2018, a promising London-based fintech start-up entered acquisition talks with a global bank. Its growth figures were dazzling: exponential user adoption, glowing press coverage, and a charismatic founder who dominated industry panels. Yet when the buyer's due diligence team began its work, the glamour quickly dissolved. Customer contracts were stored in scattered email attachments, financial reconciliations relied on manual spreadsheets riddled with errors, compliance processes were barely documented, and the technology stack lacked version control. Within weeks, the buyer withdrew its offer, not because the product lacked potential, but because the systems underpinning the company could not withstand scrutiny. The lesson was brutal but simple: in acquisitions, promises do not survive the checklist.

Every investor arrives with one. Some carry it literally—files of structured questions covering finance, operations, legal, and governance. Others hold it mentally, honed through years of deals gone wrong. But in every case, due diligence is not a formality. It is the buyer's final defence against risk, the process by which enthusiasm is disciplined into verification. For founders, this is where narrative collides with evidence, and where valuation is either upheld or destroyed. The checklist is not negotiable; it is the grammar of trust in commerce.

What makes the investor's checklist so daunting is its scope. It cuts across every dimension of a business, from the obvious to the overlooked. Financial statements must be accurate and auditable. Legal agreements—employment contracts, supplier terms, intellectual property rights—must be clear and enforceable. Operational processes must be documented, replicable, and resilient. Cybersecurity protocols must exist and be tested. HR policies must not only exist but align with compliance regimes. A single gap, once revealed, can unravel confidence in everything else. Buyers do not want to patch holes; they want assurance that the ship is seaworthy.

The logic is unforgiving. For every claim a founder makes—"our revenue is recurring," "our customers are loyal," "our systems are scalable"—an investor will ask: *show me*. Are there signed contracts that prove revenue durability? Is there churn data, segmented and consistent, that validates loyalty? Do documented workflows exist that demonstrate scalability without founder intervention? Each claim becomes a hypothesis tested against evidence. If the evidence fails, the claim collapses, and with it, trust.

This is why seasoned acquirers obsess over documentation. It is not bureaucracy for its own sake. Documentation is proof of maturity: that the business has moved beyond improvisation and into discipline. Consider two software firms with similar revenue. One stores client agreements in a shared drive, tagged, signed, and searchable. The other relies on oral assurances and half-completed drafts. On paper, their income may look identical. In practice, the first commands a premium, the second a discount. The difference lies not in sales but in systems.

Yet the checklist does more than protect buyers. It also reframes value. Founders often imagine valuation as a measure of vision or momentum. Investors see it differently. For them, value lies in predictability: the confidence that tomorrow will resemble today, not devolve into chaos. Predictability is created by systems that capture knowledge, mitigate risk, and enforce consistency. A company may have dazzling revenue growth, but if its reporting is sloppy, its governance weak, and its processes founder-dependent, investors see volatility, not value. The checklist exists to separate appearance from substance.

There is a cultural irony here. Founders tend to celebrate creativity, speed, and informality—the very qualities that fuel early-stage growth. Investors, however, prize stability, order, and transferability. What makes a company exciting at birth can make it uninvestable at maturity. The checklist crystallises this tension. It demands that founders trade improvisation for structure, and charisma for codification. For many, this is not merely a technical challenge but an existential one. To submit to the checklist is to accept that the business is no longer an extension of self but an institution subject to external standards.

The best founders embrace this shift early. They treat due diligence not as an event but as a discipline woven into daily operations. Contracts are centralised and periodically reviewed. Financials are reconciled monthly and audited annually. Compliance logs are maintained, updated, and tested. Employee records are secure and retrievable. Cybersecurity protocols are written, enforced, and independently verified. These practices may feel excessive when growth is frantic, but they become decisive when the moment of sale arrives. The companies that sail through diligence do so not because they scrambled to prepare, but because they were always prepared.

Case studies abound. When Facebook acquired Instagram in 2012, the company was barely two years old and had just thirteen employees. Yet its systems—user data integrity, intellectual property ownership, clean financials—were already strong enough to withstand scrutiny by one of the world's most sophisticated buyers. Contrast that with Theranos, whose carefully crafted story collapsed when its systems—quality control, scientific validation, regulatory compliance—were exposed as hollow. The outcomes diverged not in narrative brilliance but in system integrity.

At its deepest level, the checklist represents a philosophical demand: prove continuity. Can this company survive the founder's absence? Can its promises outlive its current circumstances? Systems are the answer to these questions, and the checklist is the test. What makes it unsettling is its relentlessness: no matter how innovative, no matter how inspiring, no business escapes the cold audit of transferability.

For the founder, the challenge is both practical and psychological. Practically, it requires relentless organisation, documentation, and systematisation long before a sale is imminent. Psychologically, it requires accepting that investors are not swayed by passion alone. They are stewards of capital, accountable to risk, and their trust must be earned in the most tangible of ways.

Which raises the final, unsettling question: if your business were subjected to an investor's checklist tomorrow, how many boxes would be ticked—and how many would be exposed as empty promises?

Chapter 4
Building Investor Readiness

In 2019, a mid-sized European logistics firm entered advanced talks with a consortium of private equity buyers. On the surface, everything looked promising: revenues were strong, customer contracts long-term, and the sector attractive. But when the buyers began their due diligence, cracks appeared. Employment contracts were inconsistent, compliance documentation was incomplete, and financial statements carried unexplained anomalies. What might have been a smooth acquisition devolved into suspicion and delay. The deal eventually collapsed, not because the company lacked potential, but because its inner workings could not withstand the unforgiving scrutiny of investors. The tragedy is that all of it was avoidable.

Every founder dreams of the moment their business is evaluated and found worthy of investment or acquisition. Yet too many treat investor readiness as a sprint, something to be addressed in a flurry of activity once a buyer is at the door. The reality is more demanding: readiness is not an event but a discipline, a way of running a company from day one. Investors do not want to buy businesses hastily dressed for sale. They want to buy companies that have been living in readiness, whose practices are not theatre but habit.

This chapter turns the spotlight on that discipline. It examines the mechanics of readiness—documentation, financial transparency, compliance—and shows why these seemingly mundane practices form the backbone of investor confidence. To the founder, paperwork and audits may feel like distractions from growth. To the investor, they are signals of reliability. Clean records are not mere admin; they are a language of trust. And in the world of transactions, trust is currency.

The paradox is sharp. Founders who thrive on improvisation often believe their ability to "wing it" is proof of entrepreneurial talent. But in the eyes of investors, improvisation is fragility masquerading as brilliance. A company without documentation, without transparent financials, without clear governance, is not agile—it is risky. Risk depresses valuations, prolongs negotiations, and sometimes kills deals outright. Buyers do not want to inherit chaos; they want continuity, predictability, and systems that can survive transition.

The stakes extend beyond numbers. Documentation errors can trigger legal exposure. Sloppy financial reporting can invite regulatory attention. Inconsistent compliance practices can jeopardise contracts. Each of these is a red flag, the kind that can turn interest into withdrawal overnight. Investors know that every small gap in readiness today can become a costly liability tomorrow. What they seek are companies that have already minimised these risks, not those asking buyers to absorb them.

And yet, there is opportunity here. The very practices that prepare a business for scrutiny also strengthen its performance in the present. Financial transparency is not just about making investors comfortable; it improves decision-making for leaders. Documented processes are not just about easing diligence; they free founders from micromanagement. Compliance is not just about ticking boxes; it builds resilience against shocks. Readiness, properly understood, is not a burden imposed by future buyers but a discipline that improves the business for everyone involved—employees, customers, and founders alike.

The chapters ahead will explore these dimensions in detail. They will show how due diligence becomes a continuous practice, not a desperate scramble. They will expose the documentation trap and offer strategies for building airtight systems from the outset. They will demonstrate why financial transparency is the dividing line between salable businesses and those left to languish. And they will highlight the red flags—structural, cultural, and legal—that most reliably kill deals, regardless of a company's revenue.

The deeper question lingers: how many businesses, if investors arrived unannounced tomorrow, could withstand the light of scrutiny? For many founders, the honest answer is uncomfortable. But discomfort is the beginning of transformation. To build investor readiness is to shift perspective, to run a business not as a reflection of personal charisma but as an asset capable of thriving independently.

The coming pages make a promise: by embracing readiness as a daily discipline rather than a last-minute performance, you position your company not just to attract investors but to command respect. The question, then, is whether you will treat readiness as an afterthought—or as the foundation of enduring value.

Due Diligence as a Discipline – Due diligence isn't just a sale event—it's a continuous practice.

In 2001, Hewlett-Packard announced its intent to acquire Compaq for $25 billion, one of the largest mergers in technology history. Yet as integration began, it became painfully clear that much of Compaq's internal information—employee contracts, supplier dependencies, even real cost structures—was fragmented, poorly documented, or overly optimistic. The chaos didn't kill the deal, but it cast a long shadow, forcing HP to spend years unravelling hidden weaknesses. The merger became infamous, not just for its strategic controversy, but for how avoidable oversights in due diligence turned integration into a battlefield.

The lesson is stark: due diligence is not something that starts when a buyer arrives. By the time investors open the books, it is too late to tidy them. Readiness is not an act of presentation—it is a culture of transparency and order that must be embedded into daily operations. Companies that wait until an acquisition looms are like students cramming for an exam only to discover the questions demand lived knowledge, not rote preparation. The test of due diligence rewards only those who have been practising all along.

Consider the contrasting fate of Atlassian, the Australian software giant behind tools like Jira and Trello. When the company listed on NASDAQ in 2015, investors were impressed not just by growth but by the evident maturity of its reporting, compliance, and governance. Years of disciplined preparation meant that audits were straightforward, documentation was airtight, and risk was minimised. The IPO raised over $450 million, not because Atlassian scrambled to impress in its final months, but because it had been operating with investor-level rigour from the beginning.

To grasp why due diligence must be continuous, it is necessary to appreciate what it really represents. To an investor, due diligence is less about uncovering the secrets of a business than about answering one question: *can this company be trusted to perform tomorrow as it does today?* Trust, in this context, is not built on optimism or charisma. It is built on records—financial statements that reconcile, contracts that are enforceable, systems that can be verified. These artefacts are not ornamental; they are the substance of belief.

Founders often underestimate the subtle signals embedded in diligence. A late-filed tax return whispers of disorganisation. A missing customer contract suggests fragility. Inconsistent employee agreements hint at future disputes. Each detail may seem minor in isolation, but together they form a narrative that either reassures or alarms. Investors are trained to see patterns where founders see exceptions. What the founder excuses as "startup chaos" the investor interprets as systemic risk.

The most dangerous misconception is to treat readiness as a veneer. Hastily polished spreadsheets, contracts backdated under pressure, or hurried audits will not withstand experienced scrutiny. Investors and acquirers are not looking for perfection; they are looking for integrity. A company that openly acknowledges gaps, but has systems to track, correct, and prevent them, inspires more confidence than one that hides its weaknesses under glossy surface numbers. Due diligence, at its core, is the art of truth-telling in business.

The discipline of diligence brings philosophical depth to how a company is run. To live in readiness is to embrace accountability as a virtue, not as a compliance burden. It means running a business as if every decision, every document, and every number could one day be examined by a sceptical outsider—and judged not only for accuracy but for coherence. This perspective reshapes leadership itself. Instead of prioritising speed at all costs, leaders begin to ask: *Is this action durable? Can it be defended? Would it withstand scrutiny?*

There is a paradox here worth dwelling on. The more a company treats diligence as an internal discipline, the less it fears external examination. By contrast, those who resist the discipline often end up consumed by it, forced into panicked overhauls when investors arrive. What is imagined as efficiency—skipping paperwork, tolerating informal deals, keeping financials "good enough"—becomes inefficiency of the worst kind, as entire teams must later halt growth to fix what should never have been broken.

Examples abound. A fast-growing retail chain collapsed in valuation during acquisition talks when investors discovered that its leases were inconsistent and in some cases unenforceable. A biotech start-up, hailed for its innovation, lost potential suitors after inconsistencies in its clinical trial documentation emerged. In both cases, the businesses had value; what they lacked was credibility. The failure was not scientific or commercial, but procedural. Diligence, ignored in daily practice, became the silent executioner at the moment of opportunity.

What, then, does it mean to practise diligence daily? It means establishing habits of documentation, not just for legal compliance but for institutional memory. It means ensuring that financial reporting is accurate, timely, and verifiable, not merely "close enough" for internal purposes. It means building systems of governance that make accountability structural rather than personal. In essence, it is about institutionalising order, so that the company is always in a state of readiness, regardless of whether a buyer ever comes knocking.

This is not to argue for bureaucracy. Discipline is not the same as rigidity. The most effective systems are those that create clarity without paralysing agility. Start-ups, especially, must balance speed with record-keeping. The insight is that speed without structure is not true progress—

it is momentum towards fragility. Just as a building requires scaffolding during its rise, so too must a business rely on the scaffolding of diligence to prevent collapse under its own weight.

Continuous diligence also carries moral weight. It demonstrates respect for employees whose contracts protect them, for customers whose agreements guarantee service, and for investors whose capital relies on accurate reporting. Seen this way, diligence is not simply an economic tool but an ethical stance: a refusal to let opacity or disorder harm those who depend on the enterprise. It is, in the deepest sense, a discipline of responsibility.

If we take seriously the idea that every business is, in some sense, always for sale—whether to external investors, to future successors, or to the next generation of leaders—then the practice of readiness becomes inseparable from the practice of leadership. The discipline of diligence ensures not only that opportunities are not lost but that the company's story, when told to outsiders, is consistent, credible, and worthy of belief.

The unresolved tension is this: founders thrive on vision, while diligence thrives on detail. Vision paints the horizon, detail secures the path. To neglect one for the other is to risk either paralysis or collapse. The challenge for every leader is whether they can hold both together—dreaming boldly while documenting faithfully, building ambitiously while auditing rigorously.

For those who can, investor readiness will never be a frantic performance. It will be a natural extension of the way the business is already lived, day by day. The question is whether today's founders are willing to adopt diligence not as a checklist for exit, but as a lifelong discipline of building.

The Documentation Trap – Why businesses with informal practices stumble at exit, and how to build airtight documentation systems

In 2012, a family-owned manufacturing business in Europe attempted to sell after three decades of profitable operations. The numbers looked promising: steady revenue, loyal customers, and proprietary designs. Yet as due diligence began, a fatal flaw emerged. Employment contracts were informal, intellectual property rights were scattered across personal filings, and supplier agreements were sealed with nothing more than handshakes. Within weeks, buyers pulled out. The company was not unsellable because it lacked value, but because it could not *prove* its value.

This story is not rare. Many otherwise successful firms stumble not on performance but on paperwork. Founders who once took pride in agility and trust-based dealings discover, at the exit stage, that what sustained their growth undermines their sale. Informality, once a strength, becomes a liability. Buyers and investors are not purchasing goodwill or reputation alone; they are purchasing a documented, transferable reality. And if that reality is undocumented, the deal collapses under the weight of uncertainty.

There is an irony here. Businesses that live by innovation and human relationships often neglect documentation precisely because they trust their memory, their word, or their team's cohesion. Yet buyers have no access to those bonds. They cannot inherit the founder's recollection of a supplier's handshake, nor the unspoken understanding between partners. All they inherit are the artefacts—contracts, records, filings—that endure beyond individuals. When those artefacts are missing, the company's true worth vanishes into intangibility.

Documentation is not merely clerical. It is existential to the transfer of ownership. A company with impeccable financials but chaotic records will falter in valuation, while a smaller firm with disciplined documentation can command confidence and higher multiples. Investors are pragmatic: they know numbers can be massaged, but documented systems, contracts, and compliance provide evidence that can be tested, enforced, and relied upon. In this sense, paperwork is not paperwork—it is proof.

Consider the case of WeWork. Its valuation famously collapsed not only due to governance issues but because investors discovered during IPO preparation that leases, sub-leases, and ownership structures were opaque. What might have been clarified over years of disciplined documentation had instead to be untangled in weeks, under public scrutiny. The debacle revealed a truth that applies far beyond high-profile start-ups: a business can be torpedoed not by weak performance, but by weak paper.

The trap is seductive because, in early years, informality appears efficient. Why draft a 20-page supplier contract when a single-page agreement or verbal assurance suffices? Why invest in structured HR policies when a close-knit team already understands its norms? But what feels efficient in the short term accrues hidden debt. Like unrecorded liabilities, undocumented practices accumulate interest over time, and when the exit moment arrives, the cost comes due all at once.

To avoid the trap, founders must reconceive documentation as strategy, not bureaucracy. Every contract, filing, or policy should be seen as an asset that increases transferability. Employment agreements clarify obligations, making it easier for successors to retain talent. Customer contracts ensure revenue predictability, demonstrating resilience beyond the founder's charisma. Intellectual property registrations transform ideas into enforceable rights, capable of defending the business long after its originators depart.

Yet documentation also reflects a philosophy of trust. Far from signalling suspicion, a written agreement acknowledges respect for the future, ensuring that relationships are not left vulnerable to memory or circumstance. Where handshake deals dissolve with individuals, documentation honours commitments by anchoring them in permanence. Buyers, sensing this, read good documentation as evidence of cultural maturity: a company that takes its responsibilities seriously, not one that gambles on informality.

Building airtight systems requires deliberate design. Centralised repositories—digital platforms where contracts, licences, and compliance documents are organised—become critical. Version control ensures that documents are up to date. Periodic reviews, perhaps tied to annual audits, prevent obsolescence. It is not enough to file documents; they must be accessible, consistent, and verifiable. The goal is to create a record-keeping ecosystem that reflects order rather than clutter, so that due diligence feels like confirmation, not excavation.

The consequences of neglect extend beyond valuation. Poor documentation creates vulnerabilities that can be exploited. Disgruntled employees may challenge ambiguous contracts. Customers may renegotiate under the guise of informal agreements. Intellectual property may be disputed if ownership is unclear. Each weakness diminishes not only exit readiness but the ongoing resilience of the business. In this way, documentation is not just about preparing for sale; it is about protecting value in the present.

There is, however, a tension worth noting. Excessive documentation can stifle agility, creating a bureaucracy that slows decision-making. The art lies in balance: formalising what must endure while leaving space for experimentation and innovation. The best systems prioritise critical areas—finance, legal, HR, compliance—while allowing operational creativity to thrive. A founder's task is not to drown the business in paper but to ensure that its spine is strong enough to carry its growth.

Examples from the mid-market illustrate this balance. A technology consultancy that implemented systematic contract templates across all client engagements found that not only did its valuation increase, but its sales cycle shortened—clients appreciated the clarity of terms. Conversely, a food distributor that resisted formalising supply agreements until acquisition talks discovered too late that buyers valued its contracts at a steep discount, doubting their enforceability. The contrast underscores the point: discipline in documentation enhances both current operations and future transferability.

At its deepest level, the documentation trap is not about missing signatures but about mindset. It reflects the founder's temptation to conflate personal trust with institutional durability. What buyers demand is not the founder's reputation but the company's independence from it. Documentation is the bridge between the ephemeral bonds of individuals and the enduring structures of organisations.

The lingering question, then, is whether leaders can make the shift early enough. Can they learn to see every policy, every contract, every record not as a clerical burden but as a store of value? Can they overcome the seduction of informality before it becomes a liability? The businesses that answer yes will find that exit readiness is not a frantic scramble but a natural consequence of disciplined design. Those that answer no will discover, too late, that the cost of neglect is not just a failed deal—it is the loss of a legacy that might otherwise have endured.

Financial Transparency – Clean, verifiable numbers separate salable businesses from chaotic ones

In 2001, the collapse of Enron sent shockwaves across the global economy. What appeared, on the surface, to be a thriving enterprise with dazzling profits was revealed to be a house of cards propped up by opaque accounting tricks. Investors, employees, and customers alike discovered that numbers which seemed authoritative were in fact theatre. The scandal demonstrated, with devastating clarity, that without financial transparency, no enterprise—no matter how profitable it appears—can endure. For founders seeking an exit, the lesson is sharper still: opacity destroys trust, and without trust there is no deal.

Yet the paradox is that many smaller or founder-led businesses do not engage in deception, but still fall prey to chaos. Their records are incomplete, their reporting inconsistent, and their practices informal. A buyer reviewing such a business may find revenue impressive and margins attractive, but the absence of clean, verifiable numbers injects risk into the transaction. In the language of investors, risk diminishes value. A company that cannot demonstrate its financial story with precision and consistency may see millions shaved off its valuation, not because it is unprofitable, but because it is unverifiable.

Financial transparency, then, is not an abstract virtue but a commercial imperative. It transforms perception. Where one business inspires suspicion, another—perhaps smaller—earns a premium simply by demonstrating control. Buyers are not only acquiring cash flows; they are acquiring confidence in continuity. That confidence rests, ultimately, on whether numbers can withstand scrutiny.

Transparency begins with discipline. Consistent financial reporting—monthly management accounts, reconciled ledgers, and accurate forecasts—forms the backbone of credibility. A founder who waits until a potential sale to assemble these documents faces the daunting task of retrofitting order onto years of disarray. Conversely, those who treat transparency as daily practice create a living archive of proof. Buyers see not only profits, but patterns: evidence of stability, prudence, and foresight.

Audits play a critical role in this process. While many mid-market firms avoid full audits due to cost, even voluntary or limited reviews by independent accountants carry immense signalling value. An external audit is not merely a check on arithmetic; it is an assurance of integrity. It tells buyers that the business has subjected itself to scrutiny and emerged reliable. In acquisition negotiations, that assurance can translate into faster closings, fewer adjustments, and better terms.

The absence of audits, by contrast, raises suspicions even where none are warranted. Investors will ask: if the numbers are strong, why not verify them? The burden of proof shifts to the seller, who must persuade buyers with words rather than evidence. And words, in transactions involving millions, rarely suffice.

Transparency also requires clarity in accounting standards. Many founder-led firms rely on cash accounting, suitable for simplicity but inadequate for rigorous due diligence. Buyers accustomed to accrual-based reporting expect to see revenue matched with expenses, liabilities properly recorded, and deferred income recognised. When records are kept in idiosyncratic ways—personal expenses mixed with business, revenue booked prematurely, or depreciation ignored—buyers face the prospect of reconstructing the financial picture themselves. Few will bother. Instead, they adjust their offers downward to compensate for uncertainty.

Case studies abound. A regional services firm in the United States, otherwise thriving, saw its valuation reduced by 30% during acquisition talks because its revenue recognition practices overstated income. The business had not been fraudulent, merely informal, but the correction was painful. By contrast, a smaller competitor, with less revenue but impeccable reporting, attracted multiple bids at higher multiples. The message is unmistakable: clean numbers outweigh large but muddied ones.

Financial transparency also extends beyond the balance sheet. Tax compliance, payroll records, and regulatory filings are all scrutinised during due diligence. An overlooked liability or unpaid tax bill can kill a deal outright, as buyers fear inheriting unforeseen obligations. Transparency means not only that numbers are accurate, but that they are contextualised within a framework of compliance. The business is not just profitable; it is safe.

There is a deeper philosophical point here. Financial transparency is not simply about satisfying investors; it is about building trust as an operating principle. A founder who insists on clarity signals respect—for employees who deserve accurate payroll, for partners who require reliable invoicing, and for customers who benefit from fair dealing. In this sense, transparent numbers reflect a transparent culture. The alignment between financial truth and operational reality becomes a form of integrity that buyers, consciously or not, reward.

Yet transparency can be uncomfortable. It exposes inefficiencies, reveals underperformance, and resists the temptation to hide errors. For some founders, the allure of opacity lies in its ability to mask blemishes. But buyers know that all businesses have imperfections; what concerns them is whether those imperfections are visible. Hidden flaws corrode trust; disclosed flaws can be mitigated, priced, or managed. The irony is that transparency, while seemingly risky, reduces risk.

Practical steps to embed transparency include implementing enterprise resource planning systems, standardising reporting formats, and separating personal from corporate accounts. Quarterly reviews with external accountants help ensure discipline. Regular scenario modelling—stress testing cash flows, assessing debt ratios, projecting customer churn—prepares the business for investor scrutiny long before an exit is contemplated. Transparency is not a document produced at the point of sale; it is a habit cultivated over years.

But the ultimate question lingers: can founders embrace transparency not only as preparation for exit, but as a philosophy of leadership? To view clean, verifiable numbers not as administrative chores but as signals of stewardship? The companies that answer yes find that when the moment of sale arrives, they do not scramble to prove their worth. Their worth is evident, written plainly in numbers that speak with clarity. Those that answer no discover that even the strongest financial performance may dissolve into doubt if it cannot be verified.

The choice is stark. Either treat transparency as discipline from day one, or face the erosion of value when it matters most. What remains uncertain is whether leaders can shift their mindset early enough—before opacity hardens into chaos, and before the opportunity for exit closes with it.

Red Flags That Kill Deals – Common structural and compliance failures that scare investors away

In 2018, a promising technology start-up in London was on the verge of being acquired by a global player. The product was strong, customer traction impressive, and growth trajectory enviable. Yet, just weeks before signing, the deal collapsed. The reason was not declining revenues or strategic misalignment but the discovery that key intellectual property had never been formally assigned to the company. Developers had contributed code as contractors without proper agreements, leaving ownership murky. For the buyer, the risk was intolerable. Millions evaporated overnight, not because of the business model but because of a structural oversight.

This story is far from unique. Time and again, investors walk away from otherwise attractive acquisitions because hidden red flags emerge under due diligence. The paradox is cruel: founders who spend years building revenue streams may lose everything because of errors they regarded as trivial. For buyers, however, risk is measured in certainty, not sentiment. A single unresolved liability, regulatory lapse, or compliance failure can outweigh years of growth.

The truth is blunt. Deals rarely collapse because of declining sales alone; they collapse because of distrust. And distrust is bred not only by deception but by sloppiness. Investors are attuned to signs of fragility—contracts written on the back of envelopes, employment terms vague, licences half-complete, tax compliance inconsistent. Each red flag hints at hidden landmines that could erupt after acquisition. The cost of fixing them, or even the fear of the unknown, pushes buyers to lower valuations or walk away entirely.

Among the most common red flags is weak financial governance. Missing documentation, unexplained expenses, or inconsistent tax filings signal more than inefficiency: they suggest exposure. A buyer imagines the nightmare of retroactive penalties, disputes with authorities, or lawsuits that surface after the ink has dried. Even a whiff of ambiguity in accounting can kill momentum. Numbers that cannot be reconciled may as well be fabricated.

Legal structures provide another minefield. Poorly drafted shareholder agreements, unclear equity ownership, or unresolved disputes with minority investors introduce complexity that few acquirers are willing to absorb. In family-owned businesses, inheritance disputes often loom in the background, threatening to entangle successors in protracted legal battles. Buyers do not pay for headaches; they pay for clarity. When ownership is contested, clarity evaporates.

Employment practices are equally fraught. Informal arrangements—contractors without agreements, staff without clear job descriptions, or unpaid overtime—may feel manageable in a small business, but in due diligence they ring alarm bells. Labour disputes are expensive, unpredictable, and reputationally damaging. Buyers see not a loyal team but a ticking bomb of claims. Worse still, when key employees are not bound by enforceable contracts, buyers fear they will leave, taking customers or trade secrets with them.

Intellectual property is perhaps the most devastating red flag. A brand built over decades can crumble in value if trademarks are unregistered, patents challenged, or software ownership unclear. Buyers know that without secure IP, there is no moat, no transferability, no enduring value. In an economy where intangible assets often outweigh physical ones, failing to secure intellectual property is not merely careless—it is fatal.

Regulatory compliance introduces subtler risks. In industries such as healthcare, finance, or food, compliance failures can lead not just to fines but to licence revocation. A small breach of safety protocols, a missed audit, or incomplete certifications may seem minor to a founder, but to a buyer it signals systemic weakness. Acquiring such a business could mean inheriting years of hidden liabilities. Buyers prefer to walk away than gamble with regulators.

Cultural red flags are harder to quantify but no less real. A toxic internal environment—evidenced by high turnover, lawsuits, or poor Glassdoor reviews—raises doubts about sustainability. Numbers may be strong today, but investors fear tomorrow's exodus. Similarly, founders who dominate decision-making without a functioning management team raise questions of continuity. If the business collapses without the founder, buyers see an asset that cannot truly be acquired.

Underlying these risks is a philosophical reality: buyers purchase certainty, not potential. A founder may present growth forecasts, visionary plans, and market opportunities, but if the foundation is unstable, investors discount the dream. Due diligence, at its heart, is an exercise in trust-building. Each red flag diminishes that trust. Enough of them, and even the most attractive financials cannot compensate.

The sobering truth is that many red flags are avoidable. They do not arise from malice but from neglect. Informality feels harmless in the early days, when speed and improvisation are virtues. Founders convince themselves that formal agreements, detailed compliance, or structured governance can wait until scale. But by the time investors arrive, informality has hardened into liability. Buyers, unlike founders, have no tolerance for risk born of negligence.

Consider the irony: the very traits that fuel entrepreneurial success—speed, improvisation, risk-taking—can later undermine the sale of the business. What once looked like agility is reframed as recklessness. What felt like freedom is exposed as fragility. Investors do not penalise founders for bold ideas, but they do penalise them for loose foundations.

The central question, then, is not whether red flags exist—they always do—but whether they are acknowledged and addressed before investors uncover them. Will a founder have the discipline to tighten contracts, secure IP, clean financials, and resolve disputes before due diligence begins? Or will they gamble that buyers will overlook the cracks? History suggests the gamble rarely pays. Deals do not collapse because businesses are imperfect; they collapse because imperfections are hidden until too late.

The lesson is clear: every red flag is a story waiting to be told—either by the founder with honesty and preparedness, or by the buyer with suspicion and retreat. Which version prevails depends not on the company's potential but on its discipline long before the sale. And so the unresolved question remains: can founders reframe their instincts, trading the comfort of informality for the rigour that investors demand—before opportunity slips away?

Chapter 5
Designing Leadership That Lasts

On a winter morning in 2011, Apple's board faced a decision that would reverberate far beyond Silicon Valley: who could possibly succeed Steve Jobs? The company had become synonymous with its visionary founder, his aesthetic instincts and uncompromising standards woven into every product. To many observers, Apple without Jobs seemed unimaginable. Yet Jobs himself had prepared meticulously for this moment, cultivating Tim Cook not as a clone but as a stabilising counterbalance—an operator capable of steering a global behemoth with consistency. The succession was not flawless, nor free of doubt, but it proved something critical: even the most founder-driven enterprises can endure, provided leadership is treated as a system rather than a personality cult.

Leadership succession is often imagined as a single climactic event—a passing of the torch when illness, age, or exhaustion makes it unavoidable. In reality, succession is not an event at all but a strategy, one that must be embedded from the beginning if a business is to outlast its originator. The failure to design for continuity is one of the most common reasons once-thriving companies falter. Where leadership pipelines are neglected, transitions become crises; where they are nurtured, transitions become competitive advantages.

Here lies a paradox. Entrepreneurs are trained to cling tightly to their ventures, pouring identity, energy, and ego into their creation. The very tenacity that drives growth in the early years often becomes a liability later. Founders may see delegation as dilution, succession as surrender. Yet investors and acquirers see precisely the opposite: a company whose value depends on one individual is fragile, even unsellable. The ability to replace leadership without breaking the enterprise is not an admission of weakness—it is the ultimate measure of strength.

The durability of leadership systems has shaped the fortunes of enterprises across centuries. The Venetian trading houses of the Renaissance, whose fortunes spanned generations, built elaborate apprenticeship and governance structures to ensure no single death or departure could sink the venture. In contrast, countless modern start-ups have collapsed when charismatic founders refused to share authority, leaving their businesses vulnerable the moment they faltered. History whispers a lesson in continuity: personality inspires, but process endures.

This chapter examines leadership succession not as an afterthought but as a design principle. It will confront the ego challenge head-on: the difficulty of releasing control without losing vision. It will explore the anatomy of teams that can outlast the founder, highlighting case studies of businesses where leadership transition preserved value rather than destroyed it. And it will grapple with the hardest question of all—timing. When should a founder step aside, and how can they do so without undermining their life's work?

To frame leadership in this way is to reframe entrepreneurship itself. Founders must decide whether they wish to be indispensable operators or enduring architects. The difference is more than semantic: it determines whether their business becomes a legacy or a cautionary tale. As you read on, consider this unsettling but vital question: if you were forced to step away tomorrow, would your company survive you—or would it die in your shadow?

Succession as Strategy

When Akio Morita, co-founder of Sony, stepped aside in the 1990s, the company entered a long period of strategic drift. Despite decades of innovation, the absence of a clear succession pipeline left a leadership vacuum that no single successor could fill. In contrast, General Electric under Jack Welch had prepared not one but several potential heirs, each rigorously tested and groomed for the top role. The eventual appointment of Jeffrey Immelt may have been debated, but the process itself demonstrated an institutional commitment to continuity. Two global giants, two very different approaches—one reactive, the other deliberate. The lesson is stark: leadership transitions are either designed or endured, and the difference often decides whether a business endures.

Succession is too often treated as a contingency plan, something to be drafted in the shadows when illness or resignation forces the matter. Yet this framing is itself the problem. Succession is not a fire escape; it is part of the architecture. When built into the foundations of a company, it does more than replace individuals—it preserves momentum, stabilises culture, and signals resilience to investors and employees alike. The companies that endure across decades and generations are rarely those with the most dazzling products or flamboyant founders; they are the ones that treat leadership as a renewable resource.

The paradox is that the very energy that fuels entrepreneurial beginnings—visionary drive, personal charisma, appetite for risk—can also be the seed of fragility. A business centred too tightly on its founder is, by definition, brittle. Its strengths are indivisible from one personality. To design succession from the outset is to confront this paradox directly: the aim is not to diminish the founder's role but to ensure their influence becomes embedded in systems, values, and talent pipelines rather than tethered to a single office.

Modern case studies reinforce this principle. Starbucks faced an existential challenge when Howard Schultz first stepped down in 2000. The brand floundered under leaders who lacked his instinct for culture and customer experience. When Schultz returned in 2008, he found a company adrift, and while he revived it, the episode underscored the dangers of weak succession design. By contrast, Unilever has cultivated a long tradition of leadership pipelines, promoting CEOs from within and preparing them years in advance. This internal continuity has allowed the company to pivot across industries and markets without losing strategic coherence. Investors notice such patterns: they are reassured by evidence that leadership change does not equate to instability.

Succession as strategy requires deliberate mechanisms. Identifying high-potential talent is only the beginning. Organisations must craft developmental journeys—rotations across functions, exposure to international markets, assignments in both growth and crisis contexts. These experiences do more than sharpen skills; they test character, judgement, and resilience. A pipeline is not simply a queue of ambitious managers; it is a crucible where future leaders are shaped in the fire of real responsibility.

Yet designing succession is not solely a technical exercise. It raises questions of power and ego. Founders, particularly, may struggle with the notion that someone else could embody their vision. Handing over decision-making feels like dilution. But seen differently, succession is the highest expression of stewardship. It transforms the founder from operator into architect, from hero to builder of a stage on which many others can perform. This reframing is both practical and philosophical: practical, because it reassures investors; philosophical, because it elevates leadership from personal possession to shared legacy.

The financial implications are equally profound. A business with a visible and credible leadership pipeline reduces perceived risk, which translates directly into valuation.

Private equity firms, in particular, scrutinise management continuity during due diligence. They ask: what happens if the founder disappears? If the answer is chaos, the price falls—or the deal dies. If the answer is a ready, proven team, the price rises. Leadership pipelines, therefore, are not abstract ideals but concrete value drivers.

There are, of course, tensions. Should companies prioritise grooming internal successors, who embody culture but may lack fresh perspective, or external recruits, who bring new energy but risk cultural disruption? The answer is rarely either-or. The most resilient organisations cultivate both: deep internal pipelines and the capacity to integrate external leadership when needed. Balance, not dogma, is the hallmark of strategic succession.

Philosophically, succession planning invites reflection on a deeper question: what does it mean for a business to endure? Is it merely continuity of revenue and products, or continuity of values and purpose? If the latter, then succession is not simply about choosing a new chief executive but about institutionalising a worldview. This is why companies like Johnson & Johnson, with its Credo guiding generations of leaders, or Toyota, with its emphasis on kaizen, often navigate leadership transitions more smoothly. The foundation is cultural, not merely structural.

Succession, then, is less about replacing leaders than about designing an organism capable of regeneration. Just as biological systems rely on reproduction for survival, organisational systems rely on succession for resilience.

Both are fraught with risk, yet both are indispensable. The founder who neglects succession effectively writes an expiry date into their company's DNA.

The question is not whether succession will happen—it will. The only real question is whether it will unfold by design or by default. And in that distinction lies the difference between businesses that flicker briefly and those that become institutions. To build with succession in mind is to embrace a paradoxical humility: to accept that the truest measure of one's leadership is not how indispensable one becomes, but how unnecessary. The lingering question for every founder is therefore this: are you building a company that depends on your presence, or one that proves your presence was only the beginning?

The Ego Challenge

In 2000, when Bill Gates formally stepped aside as chief executive of Microsoft, handing the reins to Steve Ballmer, the move was heralded as one of the most visible acts of founder succession in modern corporate history. Gates had built the company from a scrappy start-up into a global powerhouse, and yet, at the moment of transition, he demonstrated something many founders struggle to master: the willingness to let others lead. But even Gates did not walk away entirely. He remained chairman and later, chief software architect, a duality that reflected the paradox at the heart of this subject. Founders are asked to release control without extinguishing vision, to diminish their operational presence without abandoning their identity as originators. Few find this balance easy.

The problem is not technical—it is profoundly psychological. Founders often conflate themselves with their companies, perceiving organisational success as an extension of personal worth. The boardroom becomes an inner sanctum, every process an echo of their own preferences, every victory a validation of their instincts. To be asked to step back feels less like a business necessity and more like an existential threat. After all, if the founder is no longer indispensable, what does that say about their unique role in the company's creation? This collision between ego and enterprise is one of the most delicate, and decisive, moments in the lifecycle of any business.

Psychologists would describe the founder's dilemma as a clash between identity fusion and detachment. Identity fusion is the state in which the individual's sense of self is inextricably tied to the collective—in this case, the company. Such fusion provides extraordinary drive in the early stages, when sleepless nights and improbable risks are fuelled by a belief that *I am the company*. But over time, the very same fusion becomes a liability. When investors or successors demand systems over instincts, founders often resist, fearing that depersonalisation equals decline. The paradox is clear: the ego that built the company is the same ego that can prevent it from growing beyond its originator.

Case studies abound. Elon Musk, for example, has famously refused to relinquish operational command across his ventures, often creating bottlenecks where vision collides with execution. By contrast, Larry Page and Sergey Brin of Google understood early the limits of their operational strengths, bringing in Eric Schmidt as chief executive while they maintained strategic oversight. The company flourished because the founders recognised that sharing power was not surrender, but leverage. What distinguishes success stories from failures is not the absence of ego, but the discipline to channel it into stewardship rather than control.

Releasing control does not mean abandoning vision. The art lies in transference. A founder who can articulate a clear philosophy, codify core values, and embed decision-making principles into the organisation leaves behind something enduring. This process transforms vision from private intuition into collective practice. It is what enabled companies like Walt Disney to outlast their creators. Disney's ethos of storytelling and innovation was institutionalised so thoroughly that leadership transitions, however imperfect, did not erode its essence. Ego was transmuted into culture.

Yet, the challenge remains deeply human. To hand over authority is to confront vulnerability. Many founders fear irrelevance, a gnawing sense that once the spotlight shifts, their contributions will be forgotten. Others fear misinterpretation—that successors will dilute or distort the original dream. Both anxieties are legitimate, but neither is insurmountable. They demand a reframing: influence does not end with authority. In fact, the most profound influence often begins when authority is ceded, because vision is tested on whether it can thrive in the hands of others.

Investors observe this dynamic with sharp eyes. A founder unwilling to delegate is a warning sign. It suggests fragility, a business tethered to one person's bandwidth. On the other hand, a founder who gracefully transitions to a role of mentorship and strategic oversight signals resilience. They project maturity, not just of character but of the company itself. The willingness to let others lead is not just a personal victory—it is a financial asset. It translates into higher valuations, smoother negotiations, and greater confidence that the enterprise will survive beyond its originator.

The ego challenge, then, is not about suppression but about transcendence. The task is to elevate one's role from operator to guardian, from owner of every decision to curator of a legacy. This requires emotional intelligence, self-awareness, and, often, external coaching or advisory support. Some of the most effective founders surround themselves with truth-tellers—trusted advisors who can puncture illusions and provide the perspective ego resists.

Philosophically, this raises a deeper question: what is the true measure of a founder's greatness? Is it their ability to dominate every decision, or their ability to create a stage on which others can excel? If leadership is a form of authorship, then the ultimate proof of authorship is not how tightly one clings to the pen, but how widely the story can be told once it has left one's hands.

And so the unresolved tension remains. Every founder must ask: will I be remembered as the indispensable hero whose company faltered once I left, or as the architect of a structure so sound that others could expand it further than I ever imagined? The answer depends not on charisma, nor even on vision, but on whether ego can be transformed from a cage into a compass. The question is not whether the founder can lead—but whether they can allow leadership itself to outgrow them.

Teams That Outlast the Founder

In 1955, Walt Disney stood before his staff and reminded them that Disneyland was never meant to be finished. He knew the park would long outlive him, and its future depended not on his personal imagination but on a team capable of carrying the dream forward. When he died a decade later, many feared the empire would collapse without its visionary. Instead, Disneyland expanded globally, the brand flourished, and Disney's legacy endured—not because the founder stayed, but because the company had cultivated leaders who could keep building once he was gone.

The paradox is striking. We often celebrate the myth of the lone genius—the Steve Jobs, the Oprah Winfrey, the Henry Ford. Yet in every enduring enterprise, the truth reveals itself: one individual, however brilliant, cannot shoulder eternity. Organisations that thrive across decades do so because they invest early in teams, not just products. The mythos of the founder may ignite the flame, but it is the architecture of management—robust, aligned, and resilient—that keeps it burning.

This truth has played out repeatedly across industries. Consider Procter & Gamble. The company's success across nearly two centuries cannot be traced to a single figurehead but to a deliberate system of leadership development. Future executives are identified, rotated through diverse functions, and groomed for responsibility long before crisis arrives. When one leader departs, another steps in seamlessly, not as a disruptor but as a custodian of continuity. Investors prize this consistency because it signals that value is not hostage to a single personality.

Contrast this with businesses where the founder's shadow looms too large. WeWork under Adam Neumann is a cautionary tale. The company's valuation crumbled in part because its governance revolved around the founder's charisma rather than an independent, disciplined team. Once faith in Neumann collapsed, so did confidence in the enterprise. Investors saw not a company, but a personality cult, unsustainable in the long run. The lesson is stark: without distributed leadership, businesses built on vision alone rarely endure.

Case studies of endurance often reveal a pattern of intentional decentralisation. At Unilever, leadership succession is treated as both a science and an art. Rigorous evaluation frameworks ensure that talent is tested not only on technical expertise but on values alignment and adaptability. Similarly, in the technology sector, Intel's long run of stability across the 1980s and 1990s owed much to its disciplined rotation of leadership. Each incoming chief executive was steeped in the company's culture yet equipped to interpret challenges afresh. The founder's role diminished, but the company's resilience strengthened.

What distinguishes teams that outlast founders is not merely skill, but trust. A founder who creates conditions for others to lead demonstrates a rare humility: the recognition that legacy is preserved not by control but by empowerment. When Howard Schultz stepped down from Starbucks (the first time, in 2000), he left behind a strong executive team that could sustain the brand's trajectory. The subsequent challenges the company faced in his absence illustrate another nuance: even well-prepared teams require periodic recalibration. Succession is not a single event but an ongoing discipline.

There is also a philosophical dimension. Founders often believe that their intuition is irreplaceable. In reality, intuition can be codified into principles, and principles can be taught. Values-driven leadership pipelines institutionalise what was once instinctive. Johnson & Johnson's famous "Credo," drafted in 1943, outlived generations of leaders and served as a moral compass during crises, from product recalls to global expansions. Here, culture is the bridge between founder and future, ensuring the company's spirit survives the founder's absence.

Yet the ego of the founder remains the great obstacle. To build teams that endure requires relinquishing the illusion of indispensability. It requires recognising that the highest form of leadership is not the refusal to step aside but the preparation of others to succeed. For investors, nothing signals durability more than a management team capable of acting decisively without constant founder intervention. It proves that the business is transferable, sustainable, and truly independent.

Still, a lingering tension persists. In building a team that can thrive without them, founders confront a haunting possibility: that their companies may one day be greater without them. For some, this is a wound to pride; for others, it is the ultimate vindication. Which interpretation prevails determines not only the quality of succession but the shape of legacy itself.

The deeper question lingers for every entrepreneur: will your company's value dissolve the moment you step away, or will it multiply in the hands of others? Teams that outlast their founders provide the only credible answer. But cultivating such teams requires foresight, patience, and the courage to loosen one's grip on power. The founder must ask, not how long they can remain at the helm, but whether they have built a crew capable of sailing on without them. And in that uncomfortable space lies the defining measure of true leadership.

When to Step Aside

In October 2000, Bill Gates made a decision that stunned many observers. Having built Microsoft into one of the most powerful companies in the world, he announced he would step down as chief executive and hand the reins to Steve Ballmer. Gates did not vanish—he remained chairman and chief software architect—but he recognised that Microsoft's future growth required a different kind of leadership. The timing was deliberate: the company was at the height of its market dominance, but also entering a new era of antitrust scrutiny and shifting technologies. By stepping aside when he did, Gates preserved both shareholder value and Microsoft's institutional stability. The move demonstrated a hard truth often ignored in entrepreneurial circles: the most decisive act of leadership may be knowing when to let go.

Founders face a paradox that is as old as leadership itself. The qualities that drive them to create—vision, control, relentless energy—are the very ones that can blind them to the moment when they should retreat. Stepping aside too early can starve a company of the very momentum it needs to mature. But clinging too long can suffocate innovation, deter investors, and depress valuation. Timing, then, is not a matter of instinct or ego but of strategic calculation, informed by both internal readiness and external context.

Investors see transition through a pragmatic lens. They assess whether leadership continuity will sustain value or whether the founder's presence has become a liability. Buyers often worry that a founder who lingers too long will distort the handover process, unsettling employees and customers alike. They also worry about overdependence: if the founder is seen as irreplaceable, the company's valuation weakens because risk is concentrated in one individual. Conversely, a founder who exits abruptly without preparing successors risks signalling instability. Striking the right balance is essential, and it is measured not in years served but in systems built and trust distributed.

History offers stark contrasts. At Apple, Steve Jobs' second departure in 2011 was carefully choreographed, with Tim Cook already deeply embedded in the company's culture and operations. Cook was not a visionary in Jobs' mould, but he was a master operator, capable of scaling Apple's supply chain and sustaining its profitability. The handover reassured markets and propelled Apple to unprecedented value. By contrast, at BlackBerry, the founders Mike Lazaridis and Jim Balsillie clung to power well beyond the company's peak. Their inability to read the timing of leadership transition contributed to BlackBerry's precipitous decline, a cautionary tale of how delay can convert strength into fragility.

Philosophically, the moment of stepping aside forces the founder to wrestle with legacy. Is leadership an act of possession, or is it stewardship? If stewardship, then the duty of the founder is not to remain at the helm indefinitely but to ensure continuity of purpose. This demands honest reflection: is the organisation still growing under my leadership, or am I holding it back? Am I the best person to guide the next phase, or does the company need a different temperament, skill set, or worldview? These questions are uncomfortable, but avoiding them comes at a price paid in diminished valuations and tarnished reputations.

Practical markers exist that signal the right time. A mature, well-functioning executive team capable of independent decision-making is one. Reliable systems for finance, operations, and governance are another. External cues—such as investor unease, customer shifts, or industry inflection points—can also indicate when continuity depends on transition. The founder who interprets these signals early and acts decisively communicates strength rather than weakness. In financial terms, they demonstrate to buyers that the company is not dependent on one individual, which enhances transferability and, therefore, value.

Yet even with planning, timing transitions is rarely clean. There is always ambiguity: could staying another year add more value, or would it merely erode trust? Could leaving sooner risk undermining deals, or would it sharpen focus and urgency? The answer lies not in eliminating risk but in managing it—accepting that there is no perfect moment, only one that is strategically optimal given the circumstances.

This is the founder's ultimate test. To step aside at the right time is to practise the highest form of discipline, sacrificing control in order to preserve continuity. It is also to accept the paradox of leadership: that the truest measure of one's impact is not how indispensable one remains, but how unnecessary one has made oneself.

The question, then, is not simply *when will you leave,* but *what will you leave behind*. And in that tension—between holding on and letting go—lies the crucible in which lasting legacies are forged.

Chapter 6
Timing the Market and Yourself

In the spring of 2007, a small group of entrepreneurs in California sold their online advertising business for what seemed at the time like a fair, if not extravagant, sum. Within a year, the financial crisis erupted, valuations plummeted, and peers who had waited for a "better deal" were left with offers that vanished altogether. The paradox was striking: those who sold "too early" were criticised for leaving money on the table, but in hindsight they had preserved wealth and avoided ruin. Timing, in business exits, is never a clean equation—it is a negotiation between foresight, circumstance, and personal readiness.

Every founder dreams of hitting the high watermark, the mythical moment when valuations are frothy, buyers are abundant, and one's business gleams at its most attractive. Yet history shows that few ever grasp this elusive peak. More often, waiting for "just one more quarter of growth" or "one more product launch" becomes a trap, where imagined gains evaporate as markets shift or competitors rise. The notion of perfect timing is seductive precisely because it suggests control over the uncontrollable. And yet, beneath this illusion lies a deeper truth: exits are shaped as much by discipline and preparation as by external cycles.

The question is not only *when is the market ready*, but *when are you ready*. Entrepreneurs often overlook this dual alignment. They read charts of economic cycles, watch for sector trends, and parse buyer appetite, but neglect their own personal trajectory—fatigue, family priorities, or the appetite for risk that once fuelled their journey. An exit delayed for the wrong reasons can erode not just value, but health, relationships, and purpose. Conversely, an exit accelerated without reflection can leave a founder wealthy but unmoored, disconnected from what originally gave their work meaning. Timing is therefore not merely financial; it is existential.

This chapter explores four intertwined dimensions of exit readiness. First, the signals: the market, the company, and the individual each offer cues that demand interpretation. Second, the illusion of waiting for peak value, and why history punishes those who cling to it. Third, the role of macro cycles and exit windows—how recessions, interest rates, and capital flows dictate buyer appetite regardless of an individual company's brilliance. And finally, the alignment of personal life with business cycles—how the most successful exits are those that synchronise financial opportunity with human need.

There is no formula that guarantees a perfect outcome, and that is precisely what makes timing the hardest decision a founder will face. To act too soon may feel like surrender; to act too late, like hubris. But between these poles lies a strategic art: reading signals, weighing risks, and choosing the moment when legacy, value, and personal readiness converge. The pages ahead examine that art in depth—not to promise certainty, but to sharpen perception. For in the end, the real question is not whether you will miss the peak, but whether you will recognise the moment that is right for *you*.

When Is the Right Time to Sell? - Analysing personal, market, and company signals that shape timing

In 2012, Facebook acquired Instagram for $1 billion, a staggering figure for a company with just 13 employees. To outside observers, Kevin Systrom and Mike Krieger had sold too soon; Instagram had barely begun its ascent. Yet a decade later, as the app became central to Facebook's survival and grew into a juggernaut worth hundreds of billions, the original sale still looked shrewd. The founders had capitalised on momentum, secured generational wealth, and avoided the pitfalls of scaling under crushing competition. The paradox was clear: by selling "early", they might have left money on the table, but by not waiting for perfection, they guaranteed success.

This is the dilemma that shadows every founder. The right moment to sell is never obvious in the present. It appears only in hindsight, shaped by market cycles, unforeseen disruptions, and the founder's own readiness to move on. For every Instagram, there are companies that clung on too long, believing growth would be infinite, only to watch valuations collapse. For every early exit, there are founders who regret missing the multiplier effect of patience. The timing of an exit sits at the intersection of art and analysis, strategy and psychology.

The signals are many, but they rarely align neatly. Some are external: valuations across your sector are inflating, capital is cheap, and competitors are consolidating. Others are internal: your company's systems are stabilising, revenues are predictable, leadership is mature. And then there are the personal signals—often the least examined yet most decisive. Burnout, shifting family priorities, or a waning appetite for risk can matter more than a perfect multiple. The founder who ignores these inner indicators may achieve a headline valuation but at the cost of health, relationships, or identity.

The art of timing lies in weighing these signals not as isolated data points but as a web of interdependence. Market exuberance can amplify company performance, but only if the business has the discipline to withstand scrutiny. A founder ready to sell may be emboldened by personal clarity, yet their exit will falter if buyers sense fragile systems or financial opacity. Conversely, a company polished to perfection may languish on the market if macro conditions sour. The challenge is to recognise that readiness is not singular but triangular: the market, the business, and the individual must each be interrogated.

Examples abound. Consider the founders of WhatsApp, who sold to Facebook in 2014 for $19 billion at the peak of the messaging wars. Their timing aligned with both strategic buyer appetite and their own reluctance to commercialise through advertising. Contrast that with Yahoo, which in the early 2000s refused multiple lucrative acquisition offers, only to sell to Verizon for a fraction of its peak valuation years later. Both cases remind us that waiting for "more" often risks ending with "less."

There is also the question of pace. The modern start-up ecosystem encourages acceleration—scaling quickly, raising successive rounds, and selling to strategic buyers before market tides shift. Yet for family-owned firms or founder-led businesses outside the venture capital cycle, the calculus differs. Longevity, legacy, and community impact may weigh as heavily as multiples. What constitutes "the right time" for one founder may feel premature or reckless to another. Timing, then, is always personal, even as it is shaped by global forces.

Philosophically, the problem of timing is inseparable from the problem of human foresight. We are wired to overestimate our ability to predict the future, believing we can spot the exact crest of a wave. Yet most of life—and business—operates under uncertainty. The founder who accepts this limitation can shift the question from *when is the perfect time to sell?* to *when is a good enough time to achieve my goals?* That subtle change reframes timing as a strategy of sufficiency rather than perfection, of alignment rather than luck.

The unresolved tension remains: no founder can know with certainty whether they sold too early or too late. What they can know is whether the timing served their values, preserved their legacy, and created stability for those who depended on them. The signals—personal, market, and company—will never speak in unison. The art lies in discerning which voice to heed most when the moment arrives, and having the courage to act before clarity arrives too late.

The Illusion of Waiting for Peak Value - Why waiting for the "perfect" moment often leads to missed opportunities

In 1999, as the dot-com bubble swelled, countless founders turned down acquisition offers that, at the time, seemed insultingly low compared to their paper valuations. Just months later, when the bubble burst, many of those same businesses were worth nothing at all. The paradox was stark: in pursuit of the *perfect* exit, they lost the chance for a merely great one. The chase for peak value—an intoxicating yet phantom summit—has undone more entrepreneurs than poor products, difficult markets, or even flawed leadership.

The human mind is not built for timing markets with precision. Investors and founders alike fall prey to the same bias: the belief that tomorrow will be just a little better than today. That valuations will climb higher, competitors will stumble, or interest rates will stay low long enough to ride the wave. Yet history shows that the apex of a market is visible only in retrospect. To act as though one can *see* it in real time is not strategy but hubris, a gamble disguised as patience.

Psychologists call this phenomenon the "greed–fear paradox." When valuations are high, greed whispers that they could go higher still; when they fall, fear paralyses action, leading to missed opportunities on the downswing. The rational middle ground—selling into strength while recognising that "perfect" does not exist—is easy to articulate but notoriously hard to practice. For a founder, the challenge is compounded by emotional attachment. A company is not just an asset; it is a life's work. The temptation to delay, to hold on until *just after the next milestone,* is often less about rational financial calculus and more about the reluctance to let go.

Case studies illustrate this vividly. Groupon, once hailed as the fastest-growing company in history, declined a $6 billion offer from Google in 2010. Its leadership believed the company could achieve far more as an independent entity. Within two years, its valuation had collapsed by more than half, and today it is a cautionary tale of overconfidence. Contrast this with YouTube's founders, who sold to Google in 2006 for $1.65 billion—an amount many observers considered premature given the platform's growth trajectory. Yet that sale not only secured their futures but gave YouTube the infrastructure to scale globally. The lesson is not that one should always sell early, but that anchoring decisions to a mythical peak is more dangerous than selling "too soon."

The illusion of peak value is also fed by the culture of financial commentary. Analysts and pundits speak of markets as though they were predictable machines, charting cycles with neat curves and "inevitable" highs and lows. But the real economy is messier: valuations are shaped by unpredictable shifts in regulation, technology, geopolitics, and consumer sentiment. Even seasoned investors rarely call the top. Why should founders, absorbed in running their businesses, presume to do better?

There is a deeper philosophical dimension to this. The idea of "peak" assumes that there is a singular, measurable moment when all conditions are maximally aligned: the company's performance, the market's exuberance, and the founder's readiness. In reality, alignment is imperfect, and perfection fleeting. To tether one's strategy to an illusion is to risk paralysis, waiting for a horizon that never materialises. The wiser approach is to seek sufficiency: *Is this valuation good enough to achieve my goals, reward my team, and preserve the company's legacy?* That question is far more useful than *Could the market offer me more if I wait?*

Practical wisdom points towards flexibility rather than perfection. Structuring deals with earn-outs, phased exits, or partial liquidity allows founders to benefit from future upside without gambling everything on a single moment. Similarly, preparing for exit well before one intends to sell—through strong governance, transparent financials, and tested management teams—creates optionality. Optionality, not perfection, is the real safeguard against regret.

And yet the tension never fully resolves. The allure of the peak is perennial, woven into human ambition itself. Founders build because they imagine greatness; it is only natural to want the exit to mirror that ambition. But ambition without discipline distorts into self-sabotage. The investor may forgive a founder for selling "too early," but rarely for holding on too long and destroying value in the process.

The unresolved question lingers: how does one know when "enough" is truly enough? There is no formula, no graph, no universal answer. Each founder must decide where prudence ends and greed begins, aware that waiting for the peak is less a strategy than a mirage. The harder truth is that success lies not in finding the summit but in recognising, with clarity and courage, when the ground beneath your feet is already high enough.

Macro Cycles and Exit Windows - How broader economic shifts influence valuations and buyer appetite

In 2008, just months before Lehman Brothers collapsed, a number of mid-sized businesses were on the cusp of lucrative acquisitions. Their founders had term sheets in hand, valuations that seemed locked in, and buyers eager to close. Then, almost overnight, credit markets froze, risk appetite evaporated, and deals that seemed certain disappeared. Many of those businesses would not see comparable offers again for a decade. The lesson was brutal but clear: no matter how strong a company appears, its fate at the point of sale is tethered to forces far larger than itself.

The paradox for entrepreneurs is this: you may build with precision, discipline, and vision, but the moment you choose to sell will be judged not only by your own performance but by the tides of the wider economy. Macro cycles—of credit, interest rates, geopolitical shifts, and investor sentiment—do not care about your milestones. They amplify or depress valuations, dictate buyer behaviour, and often decide whether an exit becomes a triumphant payday or a desperate clearance.

Consider the private equity industry. In periods of abundant liquidity—low interest rates, cheap debt, and investor hunger for yield—firms are aggressive, pushing up multiples and closing deals at a frantic pace. Between 2010 and 2015, global buyout activity surged as central banks flooded markets with capital. Businesses that exited during this window often achieved valuations far higher than their fundamentals alone would justify. By contrast, during tightening cycles, even stellar companies find their suitors cautious, their valuations compressed, their negotiations dragged out or abandoned. Timing, in this sense, is not merely about corporate readiness but about catching the swell of capital availability.

There is also the psychology of markets to consider. Buyers are not machines running spreadsheets; they are humans influenced by fear and euphoria. The late 1990s dot-com boom inflated valuations beyond reason, rewarding founders who sold quickly with extraordinary exits. But those who hesitated, waiting for "just one more quarter of growth," were caught in the crash. Conversely, in the trough of 2009, buyers disappeared, paralysed not by rational analysis but by the sheer uncertainty of the financial system. Founders who clung to the hope of pre-crisis valuations often ended up selling at fractions of their worth—or not at all.

History shows that every founder's exit strategy is, in part, a wager on macroeconomic cycles. Yet the challenge is that cycles are both predictable and unpredictable. Predictable in that economies do move in discernible patterns of boom and bust, fuelled by credit expansion, technological waves, or regulatory shifts. Unpredictable in that the *catalyst* for each turn—be it a global pandemic, a war, or a sudden policy reversal—is rarely anticipated. The founder who ties an exit exclusively to hitting peak valuations risks being blindsided by shocks beyond their control.

Prudent founders therefore treat macro cycles not as exact roadmaps but as weather systems. You cannot control the storms, but you can choose whether to launch your vessel in calm seas or wait until the winds are at your back. This requires not only reading signals—interest rate trends, industry-specific multiples, capital flows—but also building flexibility into your business. A company with strong systems, transparent governance, and scalable operations creates options: it can hold through downturns without crumbling, but also move quickly when the market window opens.

Case studies illustrate this principle. LinkedIn, for instance, sold to Microsoft in 2016 for $26.2 billion, at a moment when public tech valuations had softened but strategic buyers still had large cash reserves and an appetite for assets. The timing was not "perfect" in market terms, but it was optimal in aligning LinkedIn's corporate needs with Microsoft's strategic goals and the liquidity environment. Contrast this with WeWork, whose aborted 2019 IPO collided with tightening investor scrutiny and collapsing confidence in profitless growth models. By 2020, with the pandemic hammering commercial real estate, its valuation had imploded. Timing, again, proved decisive.

Philosophically, this speaks to a deeper tension: the illusion of autonomy. Entrepreneurs often see themselves as masters of their destiny, their businesses shaped solely by skill and effort. But exits remind us that we are embedded in systems far beyond our control. The same founder, with the same company, can walk away with life-changing wealth in one cycle and be forced to liquidate in another. The humbling truth is that success at exit is not only about *what you build*, but *when you sell*.

This does not mean passivity. It means cultivating awareness and readiness. The founder who studies macro cycles, who understands the patterns of capital, can prepare to act decisively when the window opens. The art is in knowing that windows do not stay open long, and that waiting for the perfect conditions is often indistinguishable from missing them altogether.

And yet, the tension persists: how does one weigh the micro—the company's readiness, personal goals, team cohesion—against the macro—the vagaries of global finance and politics? There is no algorithm that resolves this dilemma. There is only judgement, informed by history but lived in real time. The question that remains is as unsettling as it is inescapable: if tomorrow's storm is unknowable, how much of today's opportunity are you willing to risk on the promise of clearer skies?

Aligning Personal Life With Business Cycles - Integrating personal goals with exit timing decisions

In 2012, a European software entrepreneur received two acquisition offers within months of each other. The first came from a strategic buyer who valued the business generously but required the founder to remain in place for three more years. The second was a lower offer from private equity, with a cleaner exit path and only a brief handover. On paper, the first offer seemed superior. Yet privately, the founder was dealing with a spouse's illness and the desire to spend more time at home. He chose the second deal, walking away from millions in potential upside. A decade later, he described it not as a financial compromise but as the best decision of his life. The story is not unusual.

The timing of an exit is never purely a matter of numbers, multiples, or market cycles. It is entangled with the rhythms of personal life—age, health, family obligations, creative energy, even the quiet yearning for reinvention. The paradox is that while markets operate on impersonal cycles of expansion and contraction, founders live on deeply human timelines. The art of exit lies in finding alignment between the two. Misalignment is costly: sell too early and one may regret leaving value on the table; wait too long and personal burnout or life events can force a rushed, unfavourable transaction.

One way to frame this is to think of two clocks ticking side by side. The market clock moves with macroeconomic conditions, interest rate shifts, and investor sentiment. The personal clock ticks with milestones like children leaving home, health scares, or simply reaching a point of diminished enthusiasm for twenty-hour work weeks. Success comes not from choosing which clock to follow but from recognising when they strike in harmony—and being ready to act in that moment.

Founders who ignore their personal rhythms often stumble. Consider the case of a North American manufacturing owner who held on for "just a few more years" to ride a strong order book. His children, uninterested in the business, grew frustrated with his refusal to step back, while his health deteriorated under the strain. By the time he sought buyers, the industry was facing new tariffs, margins shrank, and his energy to negotiate was gone. He eventually sold under pressure, not preference. The financial outcome was diminished, but the real loss was autonomy. He had surrendered the power to choose the terms of his transition.

By contrast, founders who consciously map personal goals to business readiness often unlock greater freedom. Some prepare by grooming second-tier leadership years in advance, so they can exit swiftly when family or health dictates. Others stage gradual liquidity events—minority stake sales, dividend recaps—aligning wealth diversification with personal milestones like children's education or retirement planning. These approaches recognise that an exit is not a single moment but a sequence of decisions, each one integrating the personal with the corporate.

Philosophically, this raises a question about identity. For many founders, the business is not only a livelihood but a mirror of self. To sell is not just to exchange equity for cash but to dismantle a central part of one's identity. This psychological weight can distort timing decisions, making founders hold on out of fear of irrelevance rather than strategic calculation. Investors see through this hesitation. The irony is that by resisting the personal need for transition, founders often reduce the very valuations they seek to protect. The courage to let go at the right personal moment is not weakness; it is strategy.

There is also a generational lens to consider. Younger founders may time exits around opportunities for serial entrepreneurship, leveraging market upswings to fund their next idea. Older founders may time sales to secure retirement or to ensure succession is orderly. In each case, personal life-cycle considerations are inseparable from market logic. No formula can dictate the correct alignment—it emerges from honest self-assessment, coupled with a clear-eyed view of the external environment.

Yet alignment is rarely perfect. Sometimes personal readiness collides with hostile markets. At such moments, the challenge becomes whether to wait and risk personal cost, or to proceed and accept reduced financial returns. The answer depends on values. For some, preserving health, relationships, or peace of mind outweighs squeezing out an additional turn of EBITDA multiple. For others, maximising value remains paramount, even at personal sacrifice. The most dangerous path is drifting, neither committing to exit nor preparing to endure the next cycle.

What unites the best outcomes is preparation. A founder who has cultivated financial literacy, delegated effectively, and documented systems thoroughly creates options. Options allow for timing exits not only around economic windows but around life windows. Without preparation, even favourable markets cannot rescue a founder forced to sell in crisis. With preparation, even unfavourable cycles can be weathered until personal and market clocks align more closely.

And so the deeper challenge reveals itself: are founders willing to view their own lives with the same analytical rigour they apply to their businesses? To chart family needs, health priorities, creative ambitions, alongside financial models and market forecasts? Or will they continue to pretend that personal life is peripheral, only to find it intruding at the worst possible moment?

The intersection of these two clocks—the personal and the market—is where exits are won or lost. It is a space of judgement, compromise, and often humility. For every founder, the lingering question remains: when the business is ready and the market is receptive, will *you* be ready too? Or will your own life's timing rewrite the script at the very moment you thought you held the pen?

Chapter 7
Negotiating the Legacy

In 2018, when Patagonia's founder Yvon Chouinard announced that he was transferring ownership of the company to a trust designed to preserve its mission, the decision reverberated far beyond the outdoor apparel industry. It was not the size of the fortune at stake that captured global attention—though billions were involved—but the clarity with which he defined what truly mattered: the continuation of a purpose larger than himself. The lesson was stark. For founders, the value of a business is never fully captured on a balance sheet. Price is a blunt instrument; legacy is subtler, harder to measure, yet often the weightier consideration.

This paradox lies at the heart of negotiation. The seller brings not only assets and contracts to the table but also identity, reputation, and a carefully cultivated culture. For many, the thought of handing their creation to a buyer indifferent—or even hostile—to its mission is more painful than accepting a lower price. Buyers, too, know this; the savviest appeal not just with cash but with promises of stewardship. Whether those promises endure is another matter.

Negotiating a legacy forces founders into complex calculations that stretch beyond conventional economics. Choosing between a financial buyer, who prioritises return on capital, and a strategic acquirer, who might integrate the brand into a broader vision, is not a sterile exercise. It is a question of continuity and coherence: will the business live on recognisably, or be stripped for parts? Cultural fit, so often dismissed as soft, proves decisive in determining whether employees thrive or scatter, whether customers remain loyal or drift away.

The psychological dimension is equally fraught. Some founders wish to walk away cleanly, craving distance after years of immersion. Others cannot imagine life without the rhythms of the enterprise they built, agreeing to stay on in advisory or leadership roles—arrangements that can provide stability, or ignite conflict when visions diverge. The decision is less about contractual fine print and more about self-awareness: what kind of ending can one live with, and what kind of beginning does one want for the company?

Beneath all this lies a deeply human concern: protecting what matters most. Employees who trusted their leader, customers who believed in a promise, values that shaped decisions long before the exit process began. Negotiating a legacy means ensuring that these elements are not treated as expendable extras but as integral to the deal itself. Structuring agreements, setting conditions, even walking away from seemingly attractive offers—all become acts of preservation.

This chapter turns the spotlight on the dimensions of negotiation often overlooked in spreadsheets but decisive in the life of a founder. It explores why the right buyer can matter more than the highest bidder, how post-sale roles complicate freedom and responsibility, and what practical tools can safeguard people and principles through transition. More than that, it examines the uncomfortable truth: selling a company is not merely a financial transaction but a moral and existential choice.

The stakes are not only what one gains at exit but what remains after. And the question lingers: when the ink dries and the funds clear, will the founder's vision endure—or vanish into the logic of someone else's priorities?

What Price Doesn't Capture

In 2006, when The Walt Disney Company acquired Pixar for $7.4 billion, the transaction made headlines for its staggering price tag. Yet what captured the imagination of insiders was not the figure itself but the unusual negotiation terms: Steve Jobs insisted that Pixar's unique creative culture be protected, that its leaders retain autonomy, and that the studio's distinctive spirit not be diluted within Disney's corporate machinery. The deal was not simply about buying a stream of profits—it was about continuity of a mission, about safeguarding an identity that money alone could not reproduce.

This is the paradox at the heart of many business exits: the numbers dominate the press release, but they rarely tell the full story. Valuations can measure cash flow, market share, or intellectual property, but they struggle to capture the subtler, often more decisive elements—legacy, brand ethos, and the continuity of purpose. For founders who have poured decades of vision and identity into their companies, these "intangible" factors are often the ones that weigh most heavily on the scales.

Consider Ben & Jerry's sale to Unilever in 2000. The $326 million price was significant, but what stood out was the creation of an independent board specifically charged with protecting the company's social mission. Without this safeguard, the deal might never have gone through. The founders were not willing to trade values for valuation; they understood that brand loyalty was rooted as much in principle as in product. In a similar vein, family-owned businesses often turn down higher offers in favour of buyers who demonstrate cultural alignment, because to them, selling is not abandonment—it is an act of stewardship.

The financial world often assumes that rational actors maximise price. Yet in practice, many founders knowingly accept a lower bid in exchange for a stronger assurance that their people, their culture, or their vision will survive. To economists, this may look irrational. To those who have lived inside the furnace of building a company, it is perfectly logical. A lifetime's work cannot be reduced to multiples of EBITDA; it carries an emotional and moral charge that outlasts spreadsheets.

This tension between measurable value and lived value explains why so many negotiations become less about headline figures and more about conditions. Non-compete agreements, brand preservation clauses, commitments to local jobs, or guarantees of product integrity—these are not minor appendices but the very instruments by which legacy is secured. To the outside observer, they may look like footnotes. To the founder, they are the point.

Yet the desire to preserve legacy can also become a stumbling block. There are cautionary tales of founders so intent on maintaining absolute control over brand identity post-sale that they scared away otherwise willing acquirers. In such cases, the founder's attachment, while noble, can verge on inflexibility, turning stewardship into stasis. Here lies a profound question: how does one balance the integrity of a mission with the realities of change? Every acquisition reshapes a company; the challenge is to ensure that what is most vital survives the transition.

At a deeper level, these dilemmas raise a philosophical issue: what is a business, really? Is it a bundle of assets, legally transferable, or is it a living organism bound by culture, relationships, and trust? The former view underpins conventional valuation models. The latter reflects the experience of employees, customers, and communities. Both are true, yet the weight given to each varies sharply depending on perspective. Negotiating an exit thus becomes less about aligning numbers and more about reconciling worldviews.

This reconciliation is not easy, for it forces founders to confront their own identity. For many, the company is not merely something they own but something they are. To sell it feels akin to handing over one's name. This explains why post-sale regret is so common—even when financial outcomes exceed expectations. If the buyer dismantles the culture, if the brand loses its soul, founders often feel they have betrayed themselves. No wire transfer can offset that loss.

But the opposite is also true. When legacy is preserved, the sense of fulfilment can transcend financial reward. Founders who see their mission continue, their employees thrive, and their values respected often describe the experience as an expansion rather than a diminution of their life's work. In these cases, the sale is not an end but a form of renewal, a way of ensuring that the company lives longer than the founder ever could.

The challenge for every seller, then, is to define what cannot be compromised, to articulate the "price" beyond price. This clarity not only shapes negotiations but also signals to buyers the seriousness with which the founder treats the non-financial dimensions of the deal. Buyers who understand this dynamic are more likely to earn trust, and ultimately, to close transactions that last.

The lingering question is whether such negotiations are becoming harder in a world increasingly dominated by private equity firms and financial buyers who measure success in quarterly returns. Can legacy still find space in boardrooms calibrated for efficiency? Or will the future of business be one in which purpose and culture are always the first casualties of acquisition? The answer is not yet written, but the founders who insist that price is not the only measure are the ones most likely to shape it.

Choosing the Right Buyer

When Facebook acquired Instagram in 2012 for $1 billion, many critics claimed the price was absurd for a company with no revenue model and fewer than 20 employees. A decade later, that deal is now cited as one of the most successful acquisitions in modern business history—not only because of the financial return, but because of the strategic alignment. Instagram gave Facebook what it desperately lacked: dominance in mobile photo-sharing, access to younger users, and an engine for advertising growth. The price mattered, but the buyer mattered more. Had Instagram sold to a less synergistic partner—or to a private equity firm focused only on short-term monetisation—its cultural momentum and global reach might never have materialised.

This is the paradox of exits: the cheque may be signed in numbers, but the destiny of the company is written in the character of the buyer. Founders who obsess only over valuation risk overlooking the more decisive variable: what kind of steward the acquirer will be. Choosing the wrong buyer can erode years of brand-building within months; choosing the right one can amplify a company's essence and extend its influence far beyond the founder's tenure.

Not all buyers are created equal. At one end stand financial buyers—private equity firms, investment consortia, or wealthy individuals—who evaluate companies through the prism of returns. Their playbook is often clear: streamline operations, cut costs, drive cash flow, and prepare for resale within a fixed horizon. This model can work for certain businesses, especially those with stable margins and limited innovation needs. But for founders who prize mission continuity or cultural integrity, financial buyers often present risks. The logic of quarterly returns rarely aligns with the slow, organic evolution of values.

Strategic buyers, in contrast, tend to view acquisitions as extensions of their own competitive narratives. Google did not buy YouTube in 2006 for its profits—there were none—but because it recognised that the future of search was visual and participatory. Amazon's acquisition of Whole Foods in 2017 was not simply about groceries; it was about anchoring its logistics empire in physical space. For sellers, the advantage of a strategic buyer is amplification: the ability to accelerate growth, scale distribution, and fuse innovation with infrastructure. Yet this advantage comes with a danger: integration. Many founders discover that once absorbed into a strategic giant, their company loses its distinctiveness, becoming a feature rather than a force.

The most overlooked dimension, however, is cultural fit. Culture is difficult to quantify, yet it is often the silent determinant of post-sale success or failure. When Daimler-Benz acquired Chrysler in the late 1990s, analysts praised the strategic rationale. But within a few years the deal unravelled, undone by a cultural clash between German formality and American informality, between precision engineering and fast-moving pragmatism. No spreadsheet had captured this mismatch, but it proved fatal. Contrast this with Disney and Pixar, where careful negotiation preserved Pixar's creative independence even within a corporate giant. That cultural alignment allowed the partnership to thrive, producing a string of box office successes and cementing the merger as a textbook example of legacy preservation.

For the founder navigating offers, the challenge is not simply to weigh financial against strategic or cultural fit, but to recognise how each dimension interacts with the others. A financial buyer with sensitivity to culture may be preferable to a strategic buyer who insists on suffocating integration. A cultural fit with limited financial firepower may undermine long-term survival, just as a financially powerful buyer with cultural indifference may hollow out the brand. The most skilful founders look for triangulation—a buyer whose financial capacity, strategic intent, and cultural orientation align with the future they imagine for their company.

This raises a deeper question: what is the seller actually trying to preserve? For some, it is legacy—the assurance that the company's reputation will not be tarnished. For others, it is mission continuity—the drive to see a social or environmental purpose endure beyond the founder. For still others, it is the people: employees who have walked the journey and deserve to see their work valued. Each of these priorities will point towards different buyers. A family-run firm that treasures its workforce may prefer a buyer who guarantees job security even at a lower price. A mission-driven enterprise may prioritise alignment with values, even if it means slower growth.

The negotiation, therefore, is not merely technical but philosophical. It forces founders to confront their own hierarchy of values. Do they view their company as an economic instrument, a social project, or a personal legacy? Each answer shapes the calculus of choosing the right buyer. And there are no easy trade-offs: rejecting a high financial offer in favour of cultural alignment may look irrational on paper, but perfectly rational in human terms. Accepting the highest bid may bring short-term reward but long-term regret.

History offers ample evidence of both mistakes and triumphs. Myspace, once the world's leading social network, sold to News Corp in 2005 for $580 million. The acquirer's emphasis on monetisation over innovation alienated users and accelerated decline. By contrast, YouTube under Google became an ecosystem that reshaped global culture, precisely because the buyer invested not only in monetisation but in infrastructure, product development, and patience.

The lesson is simple but profound: the price captures only one dimension of the deal. The buyer determines what the company becomes after the ink dries. In this sense, selling a business is not like selling a house, where ownership changes but the bricks remain. It is more like choosing a guardian for a living organism, one whose future will reflect the values and intentions of its new caretaker.

For founders, the hardest moment often comes not in signing the deal but in asking the questions that precede it. What kind of buyer will honour the spirit of what has been built? What kind of buyer will amplify its potential rather than diminish it? And, most provocatively, what compromises are they willing to make to secure continuity of vision? These are questions no valuation model can answer, but they are the ones that decide whether an exit becomes a legacy—or a cautionary tale.

Walking Away vs. Staying On

When Michael Bloomberg reclaimed the helm of his company in 2014, years after stepping aside to serve as mayor of New York City, he reignited a question that haunts nearly every founder who sells: when the ink on the contract dries, do you stay tethered to the creation you built, or do you let it go entirely? For some, walking away feels like betrayal, abandoning a living organism that still bears their fingerprints. For others, staying on becomes the slow death of their own authority, as they watch new owners reshape what they once controlled. The paradox is stark: the founder is both indispensable and dispensable at the same time.

The business world is full of contrasting stories. Howard Schultz could never quite sever himself from Starbucks, returning multiple times in moments of turbulence to "restore" the brand's soul. By contrast, Instagram's Kevin Systrom and Mike Krieger left relatively quickly after their sale to Facebook, unwilling to cede their independence to the behemoth's gravitational pull. Both paths carried costs: Schultz's repeated returns delayed the company's maturation into a leadership structure beyond him, while Systrom and Krieger forfeited influence over how Instagram evolved under Facebook's stewardship.

The decision to walk away or stay on is never merely contractual; it is deeply psychological. A founder's identity is often interwoven with the business, sometimes so tightly that separation feels like amputation. The moment after the sale can trigger a crisis of self: if I am no longer *the founder in charge*, who am I? For others, remaining inside a company now controlled by someone else can feel equally corrosive, a constant reminder of diminished agency. Investors and boards know this tension well, which is why many deals include earn-outs, consultancy arrangements, or transitional leadership clauses. They seek continuity, but they also anticipate friction.

Contractual complexity only amplifies this emotional terrain. Earn-out provisions—where a portion of the purchase price is contingent on future performance—tie the seller's financial destiny to the buyer's management style. If philosophies diverge, this can create toxic resentment. Founders may feel pressured to meet metrics in ways that conflict with their vision, or find themselves blamed for outcomes beyond their control. Non-compete clauses can further entrap them, preventing not only a clean break but also the pursuit of new ventures. What looks like security on paper often becomes a form of purgatory in practice.

And yet, staying on can also provide invaluable stability. Employees, anxious about a new owner, look to familiar leadership for reassurance. Customers may interpret continuity as a signal that values remain intact. Founders who navigate this period with humility—recognising their role is to *guide* rather than *govern*—can help protect both valuation and culture during turbulent transitions. The key lies in clarity: what exactly is the founder's role post-sale? Are they mentor, figurehead, operator, or silent partner? Ambiguity in this regard is fertile ground for conflict.

The challenge is compounded by power dynamics. Buyers often want the prestige of a founder's continued presence, but they also want autonomy to implement their own strategies. Founders may want to retain influence, but without accountability to a board they no longer control. The result is a fragile balance: too much control ceded, and the founder feels redundant; too much control retained, and the buyer feels stifled. Case studies abound of founders ousted acrimoniously after refusing to adjust, and of founders who overstayed until they became obstacles rather than assets.

At its deepest level, the decision to stay or walk away forces founders to confront their relationship to legacy. Is legacy about ensuring the company reflects their vision indefinitely? Or is it about equipping others to adapt it to changing circumstances? Walking away can be an act of trust: faith that the creation has matured beyond dependence on its parent. Staying on can be an act of stewardship: ensuring the handover is gradual and protective. Both can also slide into darker forms—abandonment on one side, control-fixation on the other.

This is why timing matters. Staying on briefly with a defined horizon can prevent chaos while avoiding entanglement. Walking away decisively can free both parties to grow, but only if succession has been thoughtfully designed. The real trap lies in indecision—half-staying, half-leaving, drifting in ambiguity where neither the founder nor the buyer can operate cleanly.

The dilemma endures because it is not resolvable by contracts alone. It sits at the junction of ego, identity, and institutional continuity. Each founder must ask themselves: am I willing to watch my creation change without my permission? Am I prepared to let others make mistakes I would never have made? Am I ready to be someone other than "the founder"?

For some, the answer comes easily, sharpened by exhaustion or excitement for new pursuits. For others, it emerges only after months of struggle, missteps, and painful clarity. What is certain is that every founder eventually faces the same crossroad. And perhaps the most unsettling question is not whether to walk away or stay on—but whether one can ever truly do either without leaving something vital behind.

Protecting What Matters Most

When Ben & Jerry's sold to Unilever in 2000, critics feared the quirky Vermont ice-cream maker would lose the soul that had defined its identity. Would the grassroots activism, playful branding, and deep social commitments be flattened into the homogeneity of a multinational giant? The founders negotiated fiercely, not just for financial terms but for cultural safeguards: a separate board to oversee the company's social mission, commitments to fair-trade sourcing, and protections for employee welfare. Two decades later, while compromises have been inevitable, the company remains a rare example of a brand that preserved much of its cultural DNA through an acquisition. It is a reminder that in deal-making, the most valuable assets are often intangible—the beliefs, behaviours, and loyalties that cannot be found on a balance sheet.

Yet for every Ben & Jerry's, there are stories of cultural dilution or collapse. Think of startups where the acquiring firm imposed its systems so ruthlessly that the acquired team's morale withered, or family businesses where generational trust was squandered by a buyer who misunderstood the community the brand served. Such losses are not just sentimental. Culture drives performance, retention, and innovation. When mishandled, cultural misalignment can evaporate value faster than any accounting error. Deals may fail not because of poor financial logic but because people felt alienated and values eroded.

At the heart of protecting culture lies a paradox: values are deeply personal and collective at the same time. Founders often speak of their company as "family," yet a deal hands that family to outsiders. The task, then, is to articulate what truly matters—what is non-negotiable—before negotiations begin. Is it the autonomy of the creative team? The security of long-serving employees? The continuation of environmental or social commitments? Too often, these priorities are left vague, assumed to be "understood," only to surface too late, when the legal agreements no longer have room to hold them.

This is why cultural due diligence is as critical as financial due diligence. Just as accountants pore over books to verify stability, leaders must assess whether a prospective buyer's ethos can coexist with their own. Does the buyer value long-term relationships with staff, or do they see people as interchangeable? Do they share the founder's commitment to community, or view it as peripheral to profits? Incompatibility here can undo even the most carefully structured transaction.

There are instructive case studies. When Patagonia explored external investment, founder Yvon Chouinard made clear that any capital would have to respect the company's environmental mission. This resolve eventually led him to transfer ownership to a trust and non-profit dedicated to fighting climate change—a radical alternative to a conventional sale. In contrast, when Kraft acquired Cadbury in 2010, promises about preserving UK operations quickly unravelled. The breach of trust sparked public outrage, union resistance, and reputational damage that shadowed the brand. The difference between these cases lies not only in the deals struck but in the clarity of cultural commitments communicated and enforced.

Protecting people through the deal process requires more than rhetoric. It demands concrete mechanisms: retention packages that genuinely reward loyalty, governance structures that give employees a voice, contractual clauses that enshrine social missions. Some founders negotiate "golden handcuffs" not for themselves but for their staff, ensuring they benefit directly from the sale. Others push for continued philanthropic funding or community engagement, building continuity into the contract itself. These details may seem secondary to valuation, but they are often the most enduring expression of the founder's legacy.

And yet, culture cannot be reduced to clauses. It is embodied daily, in small rituals, shared language, and unwritten codes of trust. No legal safeguard can fully preserve this. Which raises a more difficult challenge: the founder must prepare their people for change, not simply shield them from it. Transparency in communication, honesty about the buyer's intentions, and investment in leadership transitions help prevent the corrosive whisper of uncertainty. In this sense, protecting culture is less about freezing it in time and more about giving it resilience to adapt without losing essence.

Philosophically, the tension is timeless. Plato warned that laws could never substitute for virtue; similarly, contracts cannot substitute for lived culture. Founders who obsessively lock every value into legal text may discover that enforcement is impossible, or worse, that rigidity suffocates evolution. Those who rely solely on goodwill risk betrayal. The art lies in balancing codified commitments with trust in the people who will carry those values forward.

For buyers, too, this is a test of vision. A purely financial acquirer risks underestimating the very factors that made the company attractive. A strategic acquirer who recognises culture as an asset, not a liability, stands a better chance of long-term success. But recognising culture requires humility—the willingness to listen, learn, and adapt rather than impose. Deals that succeed in preserving values tend to involve buyers who see themselves as stewards, not conquerors.

The ultimate question for founders is deceptively simple: what matters most, and what are you willing to sacrifice to protect it? A higher price might require compromising on staff security. A culturally aligned buyer might offer less capital but greater continuity of mission. There is no universal formula, only clarity of priorities. In that sense, protecting culture through a deal is less about defending the past than about shaping the future you are willing to endorse.

And this future is never entirely controllable. Even the most carefully negotiated protections can erode under pressure of markets, leadership changes, or shifting social norms. Legacy, then, is a wager: that the values you fought to embed will outlive contractual obligations. For some, that means walking away with faith. For others, it means staying involved as a cultural guardian. For all, it leaves the haunting question: can what truly matters survive once control has passed? And if not, was the deal worth making at all?

Chapter 8
Designing Backwards From Day One

On a grey autumn morning in 1983, Michael Dell began assembling computers in his college dorm room. At first glance, it was an unremarkable student hustle—cheap parts, quick assembly, a few sales. Yet what distinguished Dell from countless other tinkerers was not only technical skill but a perspective that looked beyond the desk, the dorm, even the decade. From the outset, he imagined a company that could be scaled, systemised, and one day sold or floated. Hiring was shaped by the question of transferability, systems were designed with replication in mind, and branding was framed not as a reflection of a founder's personality but as an enduring public identity. The paradox is striking: the businesses most capable of thriving independently of their founders are often those whose founders had the discipline to think of their own irrelevance from the beginning.

This principle—that success is built by designing backwards—runs counter to the myth of the entrepreneur as improviser-in-chief, adapting in the moment and carving paths by instinct alone. Certainly, improvisation matters. But the companies that become durable, that attract investors and command high exit valuations, are rarely accidental empires. They are architectural projects: every choice in people, process, and positioning is made with the endgame already sketched. To design backwards is not to diminish creativity but to tether it to purpose. It is to ask at each juncture: will this decision make the enterprise more or less transferable, more or less attractive to a future buyer?

History and modern markets alike confirm the lesson. John Warrillow's *Built to Sell* popularised the idea through case studies of small agencies transformed into acquisition-ready firms by reframing their services as scalable products. Likewise, global giants such as Procter & Gamble, Disney, and even newer entrants like Canva have thrived because their founders built companies as systems rather than personal extensions. Their enduring strength lies not in the charisma of leadership but in the codified architecture of brands, operations, and teams that outlive any single figure. These cases remind us that exit-readiness is not an afterthought—it is strategy itself.

But designing backwards requires uncomfortable reflection. Founders must confront ego, asking whether they are building a business to house their identity or to exist independently of it. This is no minor distinction: the former may deliver personal gratification, but the latter is what creates an asset that others want to buy. To embrace this perspective is to shift from owner to architect. Owners operate, firefight, and often entangle themselves in the day-to-day. Architects, by contrast, structure foundations, anticipate stresses, and build with a future audience in mind. The shift is subtle yet profound. It redefines the founder's purpose from hero to steward.

This chapter traces that shift. We will examine the architecture of exit-oriented strategy: how hiring decisions, branding approaches, and operational systems can be crafted with transferability as their compass. We will study companies that thrived precisely because their founders designed for succession and sale, not for personal centrality. And we will pause for reflection, offering prompts to help you clarify whether your current structure aligns with your long-term goals—or merely flatters your short-term instincts.

What emerges is a different way of thinking about entrepreneurship itself. Instead of picturing the founder as the irreplaceable core, we will see the founder as the architect of resilience, designing frameworks that not only endure but invite new custodians. The payoff is both financial and philosophical: businesses that are easier to sell are also, quite simply, better businesses to run.

The question that lingers, and that we will confront together, is this: can you begin your entrepreneurial story with its ending in mind, without diminishing the creativity and energy that fuel the beginning? To design backwards is to live with that tension—between today's spark and tomorrow's structure—and to discover, in navigating it, the foundations of a company that lasts.

The Architecture of Exit-Oriented Strategy - Readers learn to design every choice—hiring, branding, systems—backwards from the end

In 1962, when Sam Walton opened the first Walmart in Rogers, Arkansas, he was not merely creating a shop. He was sketching the framework of a system designed to outlive him. Every choice—where to locate, how to manage inventory, which people to hire—was made with a strategic clarity that looked decades forward. Walton wasn't waiting for the day when someone would acquire his business; he was building as if that day were inevitable. That foresight transformed a local discount store into the world's largest retailer. The architecture of his strategy was not improvised but deliberate, structured backwards from the end: an enterprise designed to be scaled, transferable, and ultimately self-sustaining.

This paradox—that the most enduring businesses are those built with their eventual separation in mind—often unsettles founders. It suggests that the essence of leadership is not permanence but preparation for departure. When entrepreneurs cling too tightly to the present, treating each decision as an isolated fire to be extinguished, they risk creating brittle structures. But when they reverse the perspective—asking how today's hiring, branding, or system choices will look to a future buyer—they begin to see the company as an asset distinct from themselves. The architecture becomes visible: not a patchwork of reactive fixes, but a design with continuity and coherence.

To design backwards is not to deny the messiness of entrepreneurship. It is to impose order upon it. Hiring, for instance, ceases to be about filling gaps with convenient candidates and becomes a long-term exercise in cultivating a team that could run the company without its founder.

Consider McDonald's under Ray Kroc. His genius was not flipping burgers but systematising people and processes so rigorously that a customer in Tokyo could expect the same cheeseburger as one in Chicago. By codifying roles, responsibilities, and culture, Kroc created an organisation where the founder's absence did not equate to the company's decline. For acquirers and investors, such predictability is gold.

Branding, too, becomes reframed. Many founders conflate brand with personality, imprinting their quirks onto the company's identity. This can create charisma but rarely durability. A buyer is less interested in the charm of a founder-led brand than in the strength of a distinct and transferrable identity. Apple under Steve Jobs offers an instructive example. Jobs's vision permeated the company, yet the brand was never *only* about him. By the time of his death, Apple had become a self-sustaining cultural and commercial force, precisely because its branding and design ethos had been embedded in systems, teams, and processes that others could continue. A brand designed backwards from the end is not hostage to a single personality; it is engineered to carry meaning on its own.

Systems are the final cornerstone of exit-oriented architecture. Without them, even the strongest teams and brands unravel. Buyers seek predictability, not improvisation. A software company with codified development pipelines, documentation, and automated testing is infinitely more attractive than one reliant on a single developer's memory of how things work. Likewise, in manufacturing, ISO certifications or lean processes signal to acquirers that quality is not aspirational but operationalised. Systems are the invisible scaffolding that converts a founder's energy into transferable structure. They may appear mundane, but they are the language through which confidence is communicated during due diligence.

The intellectual tension lies here: founders are often celebrated for creativity, yet exit-oriented design requires restraint, discipline, and patience. It is easier to innovate endlessly than to standardise. It is more exciting to chase novelty than to refine process. And yet, the very act of building for sale forces a reconciliation between the entrepreneurial impulse to create and the investor's need for stability. The architecture is not simply about maximising valuation; it is about crafting a business that is both dynamic and dependable, imaginative yet measurable.

Some resist this discipline, arguing that building backwards stifles spontaneity. But this critique misunderstands the nature of architecture. A cathedral's grandeur is not diminished by the scaffolding that supports its weight. Similarly, a company designed for exit can still dazzle with innovation—it simply does so within a framework that ensures its brilliance can be sustained and transferred. This is why companies like Salesforce and HubSpot, though driven by rapid innovation, invest so heavily in systems, training, and culture: they know that scalability and eventual exit require more than vision. They require design.

For founders, the practical question is stark: at this very moment, would a buyer see your company as a transferable asset or as a personal project? The answer lies in whether you have embedded architecture—hiring pipelines that replace talent predictably, branding that resonates beyond your personality, and systems that function without your daily intervention. These are not luxuries to be added later; they are the foundations that make everything else possible.

The deeper philosophical point is that designing backwards reframes the founder's role itself. Instead of being the star performer, you become the choreographer. Instead of building a business that reflects *you*, you build one that transcends *you*. The reward is paradoxical: by imagining the end, you create something capable of enduring indefinitely.

But this orientation brings its own discomfort. To accept that every choice is made in anticipation of departure is to live with a constant reminder of impermanence. Many founders resist because they equate legacy with presence. Yet true legacy is measured not by how long a founder remains but by how well a company thrives after they leave. The architecture of exit-oriented strategy forces us to ask: is our business fragile because it depends on us, or resilient because it does not?

And so, the unresolved tension remains. In designing every choice backwards from the end, do we risk draining business of its vitality—or do we, in fact, uncover the very blueprint that allows vitality to last? The answer lies in the discipline to hold both perspectives at once: to dream as if the business were yours forever, and to build as if you might sell tomorrow.

Case Studies of Built-to-Sell Companies - Profiles of companies that thrived because exit was designed in

In 1995, Pierre Omidyar launched eBay as a hobby project to connect people selling collectables. Within a few years, it was not merely a quirky marketplace but a systematised platform humming with activity, built to function with minimal dependence on its founder. Omidyar had embedded a structure that prized scalability, transparency, and trust—features that made the company not only wildly successful in the short term but also attractive to investors and acquirers. By the time it went public in 1998, Omidyar was already less central to daily operations, and the architecture he had designed allowed eBay to continue thriving under different leaders. What began as a weekend experiment had become an enterprise transferable by design.

This pattern—the deliberate creation of businesses that can flourish beyond the founder—is not common. Many entrepreneurial ventures burn brightly and then fade once the visionary departs. The distinction lies in whether the business is structured from the outset to be *sold*, not merely run. Built-to-sell companies are those where the founder resists the urge to personalise every decision, instead embedding principles, processes, and practices that make the enterprise durable and desirable to outsiders. They are designed with the end in mind, and the case studies that follow illuminate what this discipline looks like in practice.

Take Instagram. Launched in 2010 by Kevin Systrom and Mike Krieger, it was acquired by Facebook in 2012 for $1 billion—an extraordinary sum for a company with only 13 employees. The secret was not simply user growth but the elegance of its design. Instagram was lean, modular, and remarkably easy to integrate into a larger ecosystem. The founders had stripped away non-essential features, focusing obsessively on usability and visual experience. For acquirers, this minimalism was not a limitation but a gift. It meant the product could scale without structural overhaul. Instagram's architecture was, from inception, clean enough to be transplanted.

Contrast this with Twitter, which struggled for years to translate cultural impact into operational stability. Its chaotic leadership changes, underdeveloped monetisation models, and overreliance on the charisma of its user base made it far less attractive as a built-to-sell prospect. Buyers did circle, but the lack of embedded systems and the constant identity crises reduced confidence. Where Instagram was an asset, Twitter was often perceived as a liability disguised as an opportunity. The comparison underscores a key lesson: scale without design can become fragility.

Another instructive example lies in the software sector. In 2011, Marc Andreessen famously declared that "software is eating the world." He was not exaggerating: countless acquisitions followed, driven by the hunger of established players to absorb innovative startups. Among them was Salesforce's 2013 acquisition of ExactTarget for $2.5 billion. ExactTarget thrived because it had invested early in standardised processes, compliance structures, and a culture of documentation—elements unglamorous to founders but indispensable to buyers. While competitors scrambled with ad hoc solutions, ExactTarget could demonstrate to Salesforce a business that could be slotted seamlessly into its empire. The acquirer was not only buying technology but inheriting a machine that already worked predictably.

Built-to-sell companies are not confined to tech. Consider Ben & Jerry's. When Unilever acquired it in 2000, the brand was not merely a producer of ice cream but a vehicle for values—social responsibility, environmental consciousness, and community engagement. The founders had institutionalised these commitments through their mission statement, board structures, and brand positioning. Unilever could therefore purchase not just revenue streams but a legacy with codified principles. Even today, long after the founders stepped away, Ben & Jerry's remains distinctively aligned with its original mission. Here, the "exit design" was not about lean systems but about embedding cultural DNA so deeply that it outlived its creators.

One can also point to examples in the hospitality sector, such as Howard Schultz's stewardship of Starbucks. While Schultz himself was a defining figure, the genius of Starbucks lay in how he codified customer experience into replicable rituals: the language of sizes, the aroma of stores, the training of baristas. These were systems of culture as much as commerce. As Starbucks scaled, its identity travelled with it, making it perpetually attractive to investors and potential partners. Schultz was indispensable in vision, but not in execution—a balance that made the company sellable, even if he never sold.

Philosophically, these stories raise a profound question: does designing for exit diminish authenticity, or does it secure it? Some critics argue that planning a sale from the start transforms companies into soulless machines optimised for spreadsheets. Yet the opposite often proves true. By embedding clarity—whether in values, processes, or product—built-to-sell founders liberate the company from dependency on their quirks. The result is not sterility but resilience. A brand like Patagonia, for instance, is not less authentic because it institutionalised environmental activism; it is *more* authentic because that activism has been secured against dilution by future owners.

The temptation for founders is always to conflate themselves with the enterprise. Built-to-sell companies resist that instinct. They ask: what would this look like if I were not here tomorrow? The answers shape hiring, branding, operations, and strategy. This discipline creates businesses that are not just more acquirable but also more survivable. It is not coincidence that many built-to-sell companies also become enduring cultural institutions.

Yet tension remains. In designing a company to be sold, one is also designing it to be let go. That reality forces founders into an uncomfortable self-reckoning: do they want to build a monument to their presence or a structure capable of thriving in their absence? The companies profiled above suggest that the latter choice, though more difficult, yields the greater legacy. Still, the paradox lingers: does one ever truly design for exit, or is one merely designing for continuity, with the exit as a by-product? The answer, elusive and unresolved, is precisely what makes the architecture of built-to-sell companies so compelling.

Reflection Prompts for Founders - Practical exercises to align ego, purpose, and structure with future goals

A founder can spend years obsessing over product design, market entry, or capital structure, yet postpone the one conversation that determines everything: *what do I ultimately want from this business, and why?* The silence around that question is often deafening. Companies are built on ambition and urgency, but exits are secured through clarity. Without deliberate reflection, founders risk waking one morning to find that their company has become a gilded cage—profitable, admired, yet fundamentally misaligned with the life they hoped to live.

Consider the paradox of the entrepreneur who dreams of freedom yet becomes trapped by their own creation. It is not an unfamiliar story. The venture begins as a vehicle for autonomy and purpose; soon it becomes the very source of identity, pride, and pressure. Founders hesitate to contemplate letting go because doing so feels like betraying themselves. But legacy, unlike ego, is shaped by intentional design. Structured reflection—probing, uncomfortable, but practical—offers the antidote.

The following prompts are not theoretical musings. They are mirrors, designed to cut through noise and surface the truths founders often avoid. Each is a discipline of self-interrogation that connects ego, purpose, and organisational design to the reality of a future sale.

The first and most personal question: *What role does my ego play in this company's architecture?* Many founders unconsciously weave themselves into the fabric of daily operations—the client insists only the founder can close the deal, the brand revolves around their personality, the culture defers to their word as final. This creates a dependency that inflates pride but depresses valuation. To break the cycle, founders must ask: if I stepped away tomorrow, what would collapse? The answer becomes the blueprint for building systems, delegating authority, and institutionalising trust beyond the self.

A second reflection centres on purpose: *What is my non-negotiable legacy?* Some founders want wealth as the primary outcome; others care most about preserving a mission, protecting staff, or ensuring their brand does not get diluted in acquisition. Clarity here dictates the kind of buyer one seeks. An activist brand like Patagonia, for instance, embeds environmental commitment into its governance so that no sale can erode its purpose. For another founder, legacy may mean creating intergenerational wealth or funding philanthropic pursuits. Without articulating this before negotiations, the founder risks surrendering what mattered most for what mattered least.

The third exercise is structural: *Is my company designed for transfer or dependency?* Founders should map key functions—sales, operations, innovation—and ask, "Who owns this besides me?" A transferable asset is one that functions predictably without the founder's presence. This does not emerge by accident. It requires deliberately hiring people who can lead, codifying processes so they can be repeated, and resisting the temptation to keep knowledge locked inside the founder's head. Each "yes" to dependency is a future discount on valuation.

Reflection must also probe time horizons: *What is the alignment between my personal life cycle and the company's business cycle?* A founder nearing burnout may dream of selling within two years, but if the company's product pipeline is still immature, the mismatch could harm both valuation and reputation. Conversely, clinging on during a peak because "it feels too soon" may mean missing the most opportune window. Here, reflection functions as calibration: what are my personal needs—financial, emotional, familial—and how do they intersect with market conditions? Only by reconciling these can a founder time the exit wisely.

A fifth and often neglected prompt: *What am I prepared to walk away from?* Every negotiation demands compromise. Will the founder accept that their brand may evolve under new ownership? Can they tolerate seeing their team reorganised, their office culture shifted, their product line altered? These questions are painful, but they force clarity. If the answer is no, then protections must be built into contracts; if the answer is yes, then detachment must be cultivated early. Either way, recognising limits in advance prevents shock when reality diverges from imagination.

Exercises of this kind are not abstract. They can be embedded into practice. Journaling weekly on these prompts, discussing them with mentors or board members, or even role-playing scenarios with trusted advisors helps founders sharpen their responses. Some institutionalise reflection further by commissioning third-party audits of dependency: asking consultants to evaluate whether the company would remain operational if the founder vanished. Others build "ego dashboards," metrics that track not only revenue but also how much of that revenue depends on the founder's direct involvement.

The psychological depth of this work cannot be overstated. Reflection is not merely about strategy; it is about identity. For many founders, the business is the truest expression of self. To imagine its independence can feel like imagining their own redundancy. Yet it is precisely in making oneself unnecessary that true freedom emerges. The paradox is stark: the more a founder detaches from their company, the more valuable the company becomes—and the more choices the founder retains.

Still, reflection does not resolve into tidy answers. Each exercise surfaces tensions that cannot be fully reconciled. Can ego ever be fully surrendered without losing the spark that drove the company's birth? Can legacy be guaranteed once control is ceded? Can personal goals align perfectly with business cycles, or will there always be compromise? Founders who grapple with these questions may not arrive at certainty, but they arrive at something more durable: wisdom.

Ultimately, reflection is less about predicting the future than about preparing for it. The act of asking the right questions disciplines the founder to design deliberately rather than drift reactively. The prompts outlined here—ego, legacy, structure, timing, sacrifice—are not answers but instruments. They sharpen vision, clarify values, and reveal fault lines before the market does. Yet even with such clarity, one haunting question remains: when the time comes to let go, will the founder recognise themselves in what they leave behind?

From Owner to Architect - Reframing the founder not as operator but as architect of a transferable asset

A company that cannot outlive its founder is not a business—it is a job disguised as one. This stark reality confronts many entrepreneurs when they attempt to sell. The numbers may look impressive on paper, but if the entire operation depends on one person's daily involvement, buyers see fragility, not strength. Paradoxically, the more indispensable a founder appears, the less transferable the company becomes.

This paradox is not new. In Renaissance Italy, master artisans commanded prestige but often left behind little more than workshops that dissolved upon their deaths. Their genius could not be sold. Contrast that with the architectural firms of the same period, where leaders designed systems, trained apprentices, and codified methods. The buildings stood, and so did the enterprises. Founders who transition from owners to architects grasp the same principle: their role is not to be the keystone that holds everything in place but the designer of structures that stand without them.

The difference between owner and architect begins with perspective. Owners tend to think in terms of control—what decisions they must approve, what deals they must personally close, what problems only they can solve. Architects think in terms of design—what systems will ensure those decisions can be made without them, what structures distribute authority, what processes capture knowledge so it does not walk out the door. The shift is subtle yet profound: from centrepiece to framework, from irreplaceable individual to designer of replaceable functions.

Take the case of Sara Blakely, founder of Spanx. She built the business with an almost obsessive attention to product detail, but she also invested in building a management team and culture that could operate without her. When she sold a majority stake to Blackstone, it was not her celebrity or personality that sealed the deal but the confidence that the business had institutional strength beyond her presence. Buyers pay premiums for companies with such architecture—firms where leadership succession, decision-making, and growth mechanisms are designed to function autonomously.

Contrast this with businesses that remain personality-driven. Many consultancy firms collapse upon the founder's retirement, because clients are loyal to the individual rather than the institution. Even when revenues are strong, valuations plummet. The lesson is clear: being loved by customers is not enough; the organisation must be loved for what it can deliver independently. Architects of transferable assets understand this distinction and plan for it from the outset.

Architecture is not abstract; it manifests in hiring, systems, and brand. Hiring is perhaps the most visible expression. An operator-founder hires people to assist them, to extend their reach. An architect-founder hires leaders, deliberately choosing individuals who can assume responsibilities the founder steps back from. Each hire is not an assistant but a pillar. Over time, the founder's indispensability diminishes, which ironically makes the company stronger and more valuable.

Systems form the second expression. Processes that live only in the founder's head are risks; processes written, tested, and improved are assets. Architects obsess over documentation, codification, and scalability. McDonald's is often cited not for the brilliance of its hamburgers but for the consistency of its systems. The genius of Ray Kroc was not cooking but designing an operating model that any franchisee could replicate. That is architectural thinking: distilling excellence into repeatable systems.

Brand, too, shifts under architectural stewardship. A founder-centric brand ties value to personality, which is difficult to transfer. By contrast, a purpose- or product-centred brand embeds value into the identity of the company itself. Apple illustrates this tension. In its early days, the brand was synonymous with Steve Jobs; today, despite his absence, the company thrives because the architecture—design language, product philosophy, and culture of innovation—was institutionalised. Architects deliberately build brands that endure beyond their own charisma.

Philosophically, this reframing requires humility. To be an architect is to accept invisibility at times, to celebrate the design rather than the designer. The ego resists this. Founders often derive identity from being the hero of their story, the indispensable operator. Yet the most enduring impact comes not from solving every problem personally but from ensuring problems can be solved without you. It is the difference between writing every line of a play and crafting a theatre in which countless plays can be performed.

But this shift is not without tension. Some founders fear that in becoming architects, they will lose the creative spark that ignited the business in the first place. Is it possible to design systems robust enough for independence while retaining the originality that made the company distinctive? The answer lies in balance. Architects do not abandon creativity; they embed it structurally. Google institutionalised innovation through "20% time" policies, encouraging employees to pursue side projects that often became core products. In this way, the culture of creativity was preserved without reliance on one visionary figure.

The journey from owner to architect is also temporal. Early-stage companies often require founders to be operators: hustling for sales, managing cash flow, firefighting daily crises. But the failure to transition at the right moment—usually once product-market fit and basic stability are established—locks the company into dependency. Timing matters. Shift too soon, and the business may lack stability; shift too late, and the founder becomes a bottleneck. The architect's wisdom lies in recognising when to design themselves out.

Reflection is crucial here. Founders must repeatedly ask: if I disappeared tomorrow, what would break? That question exposes fragility and guides architectural work. Over time, as fewer answers emerge, the company becomes more transferable. At the point of sale, buyers do not merely see revenue streams; they see an institution capable of standing alone, guided by design rather than personality.

Yet even as one celebrates this architectural ideal, a haunting question lingers: in stripping the company of dependence on themselves, does the founder risk stripping it of their essence? Or is essence precisely what survives when dependency is gone—the culture, values, and vision translated into structure rather than personality? The tension remains unresolved, but it is precisely this unresolved tension that defines great architecture. The founder steps back from the stage, but if they have done their work well, the play continues—and the building stands.

Chapter 9
Freedom, Not Finish Line

In 2006, after building YouTube from a scrappy start-up into a global sensation, Chad Hurley and Steve Chen sold the platform to Google for $1.65 billion. For most people, such a payday would be the grand finale, the curtain call after a dazzling performance. Yet what did they do? They went on to experiment with new ventures, invest in creative industries, and reimagine their lives beyond the confines of a single company. The sale was not an end but a release—a passage into a different kind of freedom.

This paradox sits at the heart of every entrepreneurial exit. We imagine the sale as the finish line, the moment of triumph where years of toil crystallise into reward. Yet the founders who navigate this moment most wisely know it is not a terminus but a threshold. Selling is less about stepping off the stage and more about moving into another act—one that may be quieter, freer, or altogether different. The question is not *what did you build?* but *what will you become once it no longer defines you?*

The psychological challenge is formidable. For many entrepreneurs, the company is not merely an asset; it is an identity. To part with it is to invite existential doubt. What happens when the rhythm of daily decisions, the adrenaline of risk, the authority of leadership vanish overnight? Some discover an exhilarating blank canvas; others confront a yawning void. Reinvention is not optional—it is the central work of life after exit.

And yet, here lies the opportunity. Exit allows founders to reclaim time, attention, and imagination. For some, that means philanthropy—think of Bill Gates transforming his wealth into a global foundation. For others, it means new ventures, whether smaller experiments or audacious leaps. Still others find fulfilment outside of commerce altogether: writing, teaching, travelling, or mentoring the next generation. The point is not uniformity but plurality. Freedom opens doors that ownership once kept locked.

But freedom also carries risk. The mythology of the "perfect exit" often obscures the stories of those who sold and then floundered—adrift without purpose, burdened by money they did not know how to use, nostalgic for struggles they once longed to escape. The lesson from these cautionary tales is stark: unless founders consciously design the *post-sale self*, freedom can feel like exile.

This chapter, then, asks the questions too often ignored in the transactional heat of a deal. What does selling truly liberate you *for*? How can you separate your worth from your role, your identity from your enterprise? What does legacy mean if it is not measured in revenue multiples or headlines but in the enduring impact of how you lived and what you built into others?

By examining entrepreneurs who have walked away and reimagined themselves with grace, as well as those who stumbled, we uncover not only strategies but wisdom. The story of exit is less about contracts and valuations than about transformation—about learning to see the end of ownership not as closure but as commencement.

And perhaps the deeper paradox remains unresolved: is freedom after exit a reward, or is it another kind of test? To have designed a company is one triumph; to design a life without it may be the greater one.

Exit as Transformation, Not Termination - Selling is not the end of the entrepreneurial journey but a passage to freedom

When Steve Jobs was ousted from Apple in 1985, many believed his career had ended. Instead, he went on to found NeXT, acquire Pixar, and ultimately return to Apple, reshaping the technology landscape with even greater force. His exit, painful as it was, proved not to be a termination but a transformation—a moment that freed him to imagine differently, learn deeply, and come back with renewed clarity. It is a reminder that what feels like an end can be the beginning of a more profound chapter.

For founders, selling a business can provoke the same existential confusion. Decades of sweat and sacrifice culminate in a deal that transfers ownership in exchange for wealth, recognition, or relief. Yet the narrative of finality—the idea that this is the curtain falling—rarely matches reality. If anything, the exit often marks the release of energy, the opening of time, and the shifting of identity. It is not death but metamorphosis. The challenge lies in whether the entrepreneur perceives it that way.

At the core of this transformation is a paradox: the very act that separates the founder from their creation also grants them the freedom to redefine themselves. This duality is both liberating and destabilising. The founder who sells well, both financially and emotionally, recognises that the company was never their essence, only a vessel for expression. Once the vessel is passed on, they are free to choose a new medium. For some, that medium is another business; for others, philanthropy, politics, or art.

Examples abound. After selling PayPal, Elon Musk channelled his capital and conviction into Tesla and SpaceX, ventures that redefined two industries. Richard Branson, having sold parts of Virgin, turned his attention to space travel and climate initiatives. These cases demonstrate how an exit can amplify a founder's reach rather than diminish it, provided they approach it not as retirement but as reinvention. The sale is not a closing of doors but a redistribution of possibility.

Still, the passage is not always smooth. For every Jobs or Musk, there are founders who drift after the deal, unsure how to deploy their time or how to relate to themselves outside the identity of operator. Wealth without purpose can hollow, and leisure without challenge can suffocate. The entrepreneurs who struggle most are often those who equated their worth with ownership. For them, the transformation stalls; the termination myth becomes self-fulfilling.

Here, the psychological dimension matters as much as the financial. To experience exit as transformation, the founder must engage in a kind of inner succession planning: asking not only *who will run the business?* but *who will I be without it?* It demands foresight, self-knowledge, and courage to accept that the end of ownership is not the end of significance. Legacy need not be tied to continued control.

The deeper truth is that entrepreneurs are rarely driven solely by profit. They are animated by vision, by the desire to solve problems, to create, to influence. Exit, then, is not about cashing out but about creating space for new expressions of that drive. It shifts the question from "What is this business worth?" to "What am I free to do now?" Money is the transaction; meaning is the transformation.

And yet, the most compelling exits are those that balance both. Founders who design their sale with care—choosing buyers aligned with their mission, ensuring continuity for teams, protecting the culture they built—often experience greater freedom afterwards. They know they have left something coherent behind, and so they are lighter stepping forward. The transition becomes not a rupture but an evolution.

The lesson is clear: treating exit as termination blinds the founder to the possibilities ahead; treating it as transformation opens a horizon as vast as they are willing to imagine. But it is also a test. Freedom is intoxicating but also daunting. Once untethered from the enterprise, the entrepreneur must decide: will this transformation be expansive, or will it contract? The answer, as always, rests not in the market but in the mind.

Reinventing Identity After Exit - How founders can navigate life beyond their business

When Michael Dubin sold Dollar Shave Club to Unilever for $1 billion, he had, in financial terms, achieved what most entrepreneurs dream of. Yet what followed was less about wealth than about recalibration. He went from being the irreverent face of a fast-growing disruptor to an executive within a global conglomerate. For the first time in years, the company was no longer *his*. That shift—subtle in appearance but seismic in meaning—exposed the deeper challenge: how does a founder continue to define themselves once the enterprise that once consumed every waking thought has been passed on?

The paradox is stark. Entrepreneurs build businesses not just to earn but to embody who they are. The venture becomes mirror and megaphone, reflecting identity while amplifying ambition. Yet when the exit comes, whether by sale, merger, or transition, the founder is confronted with an unsettling absence. The emails slow, the phone calls stop, and the purpose that once structured every day dissolves. Money may have arrived, but meaning demands reconstruction.

Reinvention, then, is less about what comes next on a résumé and more about the existential project of self-definition. This is why the post-exit phase is often one of the least studied yet most critical periods of entrepreneurial life. It requires a shift from external validation—the metrics of growth, valuation, and headlines—to internal coherence: the quieter but more demanding task of asking, *Who am I without this business?*

Some founders turn to philanthropy, seeking to redirect entrepreneurial drive toward social impact. Pierre Omidyar, after selling eBay, built an extensive philanthropic network, treating the deployment of capital as an exercise in systems change rather than accumulation. Others embrace serial entrepreneurship, compelled by the addictive rhythm of building. Stewart Butterfield, after Flickr was acquired by Yahoo, co-founded Slack, reinventing himself and influencing how millions work. These examples highlight two diverging paths: one outward-facing, broadening influence, the other inward-facing, reconstructing identity through new creation.

Yet reinvention is rarely smooth. For every Butterfield or Omidyar, there are those who fall into disorientation, a condition psychologists describe as "role exit shock." The entrepreneur who once wielded authority and purpose may now feel adrift, struggling to reconcile their past prominence with present ambiguity. The challenge is compounded by ego. If one's sense of self was too tightly bound to the title of founder or CEO, disentangling becomes not just difficult but painful.

Here lies the deeper philosophical tension: should identity be defined by what one does, or by who one is? The founder who sells a company built over decades must confront the risk of over-identification with achievement. Reinvention asks them to rediscover value in being, not just doing. Some navigate this by cultivating practices—writing, teaching, mentoring—that affirm identity beyond ownership. Others engage in reflection, travel, or even withdrawal, seeking the space to dismantle old constructs before erecting new ones.

At its best, reinvention becomes a liberation. Without the relentless pressure of payrolls, investor calls, or quarterly targets, entrepreneurs are free to pursue passions long deferred. They might explore creativity, education, or activism, drawing on the skills that made them effective founders but applying them to new fields. The entrepreneurial impulse does not vanish; it mutates. The skill of imagining what does not yet exist, of organising people and resources to bring it into being, can serve as the foundation for a second or third life chapter.

But freedom also presents a danger: the temptation to fill the void with distractions rather than meaningful pursuits. Some become perpetual dabblers, spreading themselves thin across boards and advisory roles without ever re-establishing a coherent identity. The appearance of productivity masks a deeper avoidance of the central question: *What do I truly want to stand for now?* Reinvention requires focus, not merely activity.

There is, too, a generational dimension. Younger founders, like those who cashed out of dot-com ventures in their twenties, face the unsettling prospect of having "peaked" before mid-life. Reinvention for them is not simply about redefinition but about resisting the narrative of premature climax. Older founders, by contrast, often find themselves negotiating legacy, asking how their lives' work can endure without them. In both cases, identity is reframed not as a static possession but as a dynamic process.

The most successful reinventions tend to share a pattern: they honour the past without being imprisoned by it. Founders who can speak of their former business with gratitude yet look forward with curiosity embody resilience. They neither cling nostalgically to what was nor dismiss it as irrelevant. Instead, they carry the essence of their entrepreneurial identity—vision, resilience, creativity—into new domains.

And so, reinvention after exit is less a clean break than a dialogue between past and future. The founder must learn to be at peace with discontinuity, to accept that identity is iterative, layered, and evolving. The question is not whether life after business will be meaningful, but whether the individual has the courage to construct meaning anew.

The irony is that while investors, analysts, and even journalists often treat the sale of a company as the final punctuation mark, for the founder it is usually only a comma. What follows may be the truest test: can they translate entrepreneurial brilliance into a broader, freer, more enduring sense of self? The exit ends ownership. It need not end identity. The blank page remains, awaiting authorship.

Lessons From Those Who Walked Away - Narratives of entrepreneurs who sold and found new forms of fulfilment

When Jan Koum sold WhatsApp to Facebook for $19 billion, the world assumed he had reached the pinnacle of entrepreneurial success. Yet just a few years later, he left the parent company, quietly stepping away from one of the most valuable communication platforms on earth. His departure was not driven by a need for more money—he already had more than he could ever spend—but by the pursuit of integrity and alignment with personal values. In walking away, Koum highlighted a truth often obscured by headlines: fulfilment after an exit is not guaranteed by the size of the deal but by the shape of life one chooses beyond it.

This paradox sits at the heart of the entrepreneurial journey. To the outside world, selling a company is the ultimate validation. But for the founder, the exit is merely a threshold. What lies on the other side varies dramatically. Some discover renewed purpose, leveraging freedom to craft meaningful second acts. Others stumble into a void, disoriented by the sudden absence of structure and identity.

The stories of those who have walked away provide both caution and inspiration, illuminating the choices that can turn wealth into wisdom, and release into reinvention.

Consider Howard Schultz, who stepped down as CEO of Starbucks in 2000, only to return eight years later. His first departure was meant to mark a transition into philanthropy and personal pursuits. Instead, he found himself restless, missing the gravitational pull of the company he had shaped. His eventual return underscored how deeply identity can remain entangled with enterprise, and how "walking away" is often less a clean break than a negotiation between past and future.

Contrast that with Anne Wojcicki of 23andMe, who, after years of scaling her genomics company, publicly mused on how founders must eventually choose between being operators and guardians of mission. She observed that true fulfilment lies not in clinging to control but in ensuring the original vision endures, even under new stewardship. While she has not fully walked away, her reflections mirror those of many who have: satisfaction is measured less by continued command than by continuity of impact.

There are, too, entrepreneurs who have consciously redefined success in entirely new fields. Richard Branson famously built the Virgin Group by moving from one industry to another, often selling or spinning off parts of his empire while redirecting energy into new ventures and philanthropic causes. His fulfilment does not come from possession of any one company but from the continual act of creation and exploration. To him, walking away is not abandonment but evolution.

At the opposite end are quieter examples, no less instructive. Take the many founders of small-to-mid-sized businesses who sell to private equity firms, not for fame but for freedom. Their narratives often involve relocating, starting modest ventures, or dedicating themselves to family and community. The lesson is simple yet profound: fulfilment is contextual. For some, it means scaling the next mountain; for others, it means finally being able to rest at base camp without apology.

Philosophically, these divergent paths raise a fundamental question: is entrepreneurship a vocation or a stage? If it is vocation, then walking away is never truly walking away—it is a redirection of the same impulse to build, disrupt, and improve. If it is a stage, then the exit is a closing chapter, after which a new identity must be forged. Both models can yield fulfilment, but only if the founder recognises which applies to them.

The stories also highlight a recurring tension between external validation and internal alignment. Public perception tends to measure post-exit fulfilment by visibility—new ventures launched, foundations created, headlines sustained. Yet many of the most content entrepreneurs are those who recede from public view, choosing anonymity over acclaim. The lesson here is that fulfilment cannot be outsourced to the gaze of others. It must be defined privately, often in ways that defy narrative simplicity.

Equally striking is how walking away often sharpens clarity about values. Jan Koum left because he could not reconcile his beliefs about privacy with the direction of Facebook. Howard Schultz returned because he could not bear to watch Starbucks drift from its mission. Branson continues to pivot because his values lie in curiosity and expansion. In every case, the act of leaving—or staying gone—becomes a statement about what matters most.

Yet fulfilment is not static. What satisfies in the first year post-exit may ring hollow a decade later. The founder who initially revels in leisure may soon crave structure. The one who rushes into a new venture may later wish they had taken time to reflect. Fulfilment is iterative, demanding ongoing self-awareness. The danger lies not in walking away but in assuming that one definitive step guarantees lasting contentment.

The ultimate lesson from those who walked away is not that there is a single path to fulfilment but that there are many, each shaped by personality, values, and timing. What unites these stories is the recognition that selling a business is less about endings than about choices. The money may close the transaction, but the meaning emerges only in what follows.

And so, the unresolved question lingers: when the applause has faded and the papers are signed, will you carry your entrepreneurial spirit into new realms, or will you find fulfilment in finally laying it down? For those who sell, the true negotiation is not with buyers or investors but with themselves—a negotiation that begins the moment they walk away.

The Entrepreneur's True Legacy - Beyond ownership: shaping an identity and impact that outlasts both business and exit

What will remain when the company no longer bears your name? For many founders, the question only becomes urgent once the ink is drying on a sale agreement, yet it shadows every stage of the entrepreneurial life. Wealth can be transferred, titles can be resigned, but legacy—what persists after the exit—is harder to measure and impossible to buy. It rests not in share price or transaction size but in the enduring shape of ideas, values, and institutions that continue when the founder's hand is gone.

Steve Jobs' influence did not vanish when he stepped away from Apple, nor did Muhammad Yunus' impact dissipate once Grameen Bank became larger than his direct control. In both cases, legacy was cemented by the resilience of a vision translated into systems and cultures that could thrive independently. The paradox is stark: true legacy requires letting go, yet it also demands having built something strong enough to withstand absence.

For founders, this introduces a tension between the immediate goals of growth and the slower work of permanence. It is easy to chase quarterly targets, attract headlines, or engineer a lucrative acquisition. But crafting a legacy asks deeper questions: Will the organisation stand for something beyond efficiency and profit? Will the employees carry forward a sense of purpose, not just a set of tasks? Will customers and communities remember what you stood for once you are no longer there to embody it?

Legacy operates on several layers. There is the institutional layer, where governance, culture, and brand outlive the founder's direct involvement. There is the societal layer, where products, innovations, or philanthropic work alter the wider landscape. And there is the personal layer: the memory of how a founder treated people, the standards of integrity or vision that became part of their story. In each dimension, the exit is merely a punctuation mark, not the full sentence.

History offers instructive contrasts. Henry Ford revolutionised industry but left a complex legacy: innovation entwined with authoritarian control. Anita Roddick, founder of The Body Shop, embedded activism in her brand, ensuring that social responsibility remained core long after her departure. One founder's exit marked the dilution of values; another's departure proved the durability of principles. The difference lay not in market timing or financial terms but in the foresight to design culture and purpose as assets as valuable as factories and patents.

Modern founders face the same dilemma in sharper relief. In an age of fast capital and fleeting attention, there is temptation to optimise for maximum valuation rather than enduring meaning. Yet entrepreneurs who ignore legacy risk creating companies that vanish as quickly as they appeared. Consider the fate of MySpace, a once-dominant platform whose lack of cultural anchoring made its decline inevitable. Contrast that with Patagonia, where Yvon Chouinard's commitment to environmental stewardship has been institutionalised to the point that even his exit was an act of legacy: transferring ownership to a trust to preserve mission.

Philosophically, legacy raises a question about identity. Is the entrepreneur merely an owner of assets, or a custodian of ideas? Ownership ends with the sale; custodianship continues as long as the impact remains alive in the world. To embrace the latter is to accept that the business is not the final measure of achievement but a medium through which one's principles are tested and expressed.

This reframing also reshapes how we think about freedom after exit. If a founder regards their business only as a vehicle for personal wealth, freedom comes at the moment of sale. If they regard it as part of a broader contribution, freedom comes when they can see that contribution flourish without them. Legacy, then, is both a relinquishment and a fulfilment: the act of stepping aside and watching something greater than the self persist.

The challenge is that legacy resists neat accounting. It cannot be codified in a valuation report or secured in a legal clause. It must be lived, demonstrated, and embedded until it becomes part of the fabric of the enterprise and the consciousness of others. This is why employees often remember leaders less for their strategic decisions than for the daily standards they set—how they handled setbacks, how they listened, how they embodied purpose. Legacy is not only written in balance sheets but in memories.

For founders designing their exit, the practical implication is profound. Negotiations should not end at price and control but extend to continuity of culture, brand, and mission. Who the buyer is matters as much as the cheque they write. Structures can be created—foundations, trusts, mission charters—that preserve values beyond personal tenure. But more than mechanisms, legacy requires intention: the foresight to ask, *What will endure when I am no longer here?*

And so the deeper question emerges, one without easy resolution: will your life's work be remembered as a transaction, or as a transformation? The answer lies not in the moment you sell, but in the vision you embed long before. For in the end, the entrepreneur's true legacy is never the company they owned—it is the future they helped shape once they were gone.

About the Author

Jonathan Mercer writes with the conviction that freedom is not found in endless ownership, but in the ability to let go with purpose. Drawing on his background studying the psychology of leadership and the economics of markets, his work explores the overlooked decisions that determine whether enterprises endure. His perspective is shaped by a fascination with history's great builders who designed not just for growth but for succession. He believes businesses should be built as transferable assets—legacies that outlast their founders. With a voice that balances pragmatic rigour and cultural insight, Mercer guides entrepreneurs to design with the end in mind, challenging the myth that holding on forever is the measure of success.

www.ingramcontent.com/pod-product-compliance
Lightning Source LLC
Chambersburg PA
CBHW031348230926
51848CB00002B/437